THE Hobbies STORY

Terry Davy

NOSTALGIA Publications

TOFTWOOD · DEREHAM · NORFOLK
ENGLAND · NR19 1NB

Published by:
NOSTALGIA PUBLICATIONS
(Terry Davy)
7 Elm Park, Toftwood,
Dereham, Norfolk, England,
NR19 1NB

First Impression: August 1998

ISBN 0 947630 19 8

Design and typesetting:
NOSTALGIA PUBLICATIONS

Printed by:
GALLIARD (PRINTERS) LTD.
Queen Anne's Road,
Great Yarmouth, Norfolk, NR31 0LL

Front cover illustration:
Hobbies' Demonstration Car at Great Yarmouth Carnival in the 1920s

Contents

Please Note:

The small drawings inserted in each chapter heading are designs for fretwork projects issued over the years by Hobbies Ltd. Some are contemporary with the dates dealt with in those chapters whilst others come from the very first issues of Hobbies Weekly and Hobbies Handbook.

Hobbies' engineering department staff c.1923

Introduction

IN the past, the townspeople of Dereham have been fortunate to have enjoyed high levels of employment. This was largely brought about because several local businesses became well-known nationally and, in some cases, internationally. Unfortunately, some have not survived.

Fruehauf, formerly Cranes and dating back to 1865 when the company was founded in Great Fransham, was once famous for making trailers for carrying substantial loads. These were used on large construction projects all over the world; probably the most famous was the building of the Kariba Dam in 1960. This is one of the biggest dams in the world and supplies hydro-electricity to a large part of Africa from its position on the Zambesi river. The largest trailer ever built by Cranes, and a world record-breaker at the time, was a massive 300-ton vehicle on 96 wheels, which was constructed for Wynns in the late 1950s.

Jentique gained a countrywide reputation for making quality reproduction furniture. Metamec was a later offshoot of Jentique, and their clocks were sold countrywide and exported to many countries.

Whilst each firm was well-known by name, none placed Dereham on the map in the manner achieved by Hobbies. The two names, "Hobbies" and "Dereham", became synonymous to the tens of thousands of customers whom Hobbies have served for over a century.

This book does not pretend to be a definitive history, but is the story of a family firm. Just like any family, the firm has had its successes, disappointments, joys and failures, new arrivals and departures, but has retained its family virtues to the present day.

The story begins in the 1880s, when John Henry Skinner established J. H. Skinner & Co. The first products catered for the fretwork enthusiast. Wood came from the sawmill of John Skinner's uncle, William Stebbings, and fretmachines and tools were imported from America and Germany. Cameras were the first products actually manufactured by J. H. Skinner & Co. In those days cameras were mainly constructed of wood with a few brass fittings.

In 1895 the publication *Hobbies Weekly* was launched. This promoted a wide range of hobbies to an eager readership and led to a massive increase in business for J. H. Skinner & Co. In 1897 Hobbies Publishing Co. (which published *Hobbies Weekly*) and J. H. Skinner & Co. were amalgamated to form Hobbies Ltd., which was destined to become a legend in its own lifetime.

Rapid expansion followed with retail shops being established in many major cities, and agents were appointed throughout the United Kingdom and abroad. Before long, Hobbies Ltd. had become the largest manufacturer of fretwork tools and supplies in the world. Generations of fretworkers purchased designs and materials from Hobbies, first for their own enjoyment, later to make toys for their children. Many of the same fretworkers are still ordering from Hobbies, but now they are making items for their grandchildren, or even great-grandchildren.

Over the years many other hobbies were introduced to the readership of *Hobbies Weekly*, but the predominant theme was always fretwork. Hobbies Ltd. survived two world wars and economic depressions, but went into a decline in the 1950s from which it could not recover. After a take-over, the firm was later liquidated in 1968.

But the Phoenix was to rise again! In 1969 Ivan Stroulger, an ex-employee of Hobbies Ltd., started a small manufacturing and mail order company specialising in doll's house kits, which had been a popular Hobbies' line. In 1978 he acquired the copyright to the original Hobbies' trademark and designs, and once again "the old firm" was back in business in Dereham.

Hobbies (Dereham) Ltd. is a family-run business, just like the original firm back in the 1880s. The staff are proud to be involved in the continuation of a long tradition of fretwork in Dereham. However, it remains to be seen how many can achieve the long service records set by some employees of the original Hobbies. Over forty years was commonplace, fifty years service was not rare, whilst one member of staff served the company for an incredible 60 years!

When Hobbies Ltd. was liquidated in 1968 most of the company records were destroyed. Fortunately several contemporary photographs were rescued from the rubbish skip, and many appear in this book. The research for this book has involved interviewing a number of former employees. Not a single one had a harsh word to say about Hobbies. Most recalled that their days there were happy ones. Some even had the glint of a tear in their eyes as they recalled events or former colleagues, sadly no longer with us. Research beyond living memory revealed that this was not a recent phenomena, but one which could be traced back to the very beginning, when John Henry Skinner was managing director.

In the heydays of Hobbies, there would have been very few Dereham families that did not have at least one member of the family working for the firm. Even those who did not were indirectly affected by the presence of Hobbies. The whole town used to set their clocks by the sound of the Hobbies' hooter, which signalled the end of the morning and evening work sessions. Then hundreds of cyclists would throng the streets of Dereham when workers from Hobbies joined those from Jentique, Cranes, Metamec, the Foundry, Dreibholtz & Floering, and many smaller businesses, as they made their way home for lunch or tea. The last week in July and the first week in August left Dereham a ghost town as the same workers took their annual holiday, perhaps a week in a caravan at Gt. Yarmouth, two weeks if they were lucky, and, of course, travelling to their destination by rail.

Sadly those "good old days" have disappeared into history, so read on, indulge yourself in a family story of pure nostalgia!

Tony Davy

TOFTWOOD, DEREHAM, NORFOLK
AUGUST 1998

Please Note
Throughout this book, in chapters dealing with the period prior to decimalisation, prices have been given as pounds, shillings and pence (£.s.d.). As a reminder to those who have forgotten the old monetary system, and for the benefit of those too young to remember, £1 was divided into 20 shillings, 12 pence equalled 1 shilling. Hence, £1.15.0 is the same as 35/- and is equal to today's value of £1.75; similarly 16/- equates to 80p, and 6d. to 2½p.

TODAY IS THE TOMORROW
WE WORRIED ABOUT
YESTERDAY,
AND ALL IS WELL

From Little Acorns

THE origins of the craft of fretwork have been lost in the mists of time. Examples can be found in the decorative arts of most of the world's ancient civilisations. Older dictionaries define fretwork as being "ornamental work consisting of small fillets intersecting each other at right angles; bars crossed and interlaced". Motifs and patterns from the ancient Greek, Roman and Egyptian cultures certainly demonstrate this angular method of decoration, both in pierced and overlay forms. The method of cutting curved lines, known as scroll work because it represented the lines taken by unrolled scrolls, became incorporated with the angular fretwork and can be seen in the ancient art of cultures such as the Islamic, Indian, Celtic and Chinese. Many materials have been decorated in this way, including stone, ceramics, ivory and precious metals, but nowadays "fretwork" is more commonly associated with the cutting of decorative patterns in thin pieces of wood. However, Americans still use the term "scrollwork", created with a scroll saw, to mean the same thing.

The hobby of fretwork in Great Britain seems to have been largely unheard of until the Tudor period and reached its peak in popularity during the Victorian era. The Victorians were great lovers of elaborately decorated fretwork items, and nearly every household would own at least one pipe rack, clock, toast rack or similar item. Nearly every living-room wall would be adorned by at least one fretwork picture with highly ornamented lettering proclaiming "Home Sweet Home", "Bless This House", or a short Biblical text.

The first hand fretsaws were rather heavy tools similar to what is now known as a coping saw. It is thought that the first fine fretsaw blades were made in the late 1500s by a German clockmaker. These narrow-cutting blades were held in wooden frames similar in shape to the metal ones used to the present day. Although large frame saws had been in use in saw mills as far back as the early 1600s, the first small portable fretsaw machines did not make an appearance until the mid-1800s. These were foot-powered utilising either a treadle or pedal mechanism to operate the reciprocating action of the blade. The frame was usually made of cast iron to provide weight and rigidity, and the sawing arms were made of hardwood to provide resilience and prevent frequent breakage of the fine steel blades. One of the leading early manufacturers of treadle fretsaws was W. F. and John Barnes Company of Rockford, Illinois, USA.

THE ACORN GERMINATES

In the late Victorian period, in the market town of East Dereham, in the centre of rural Norfolk, a young entrepreneur realised the marketing potential of the popular fretwork hobby. John Henry Skinner was soon to see his dream expand into a business which became a household name not only nationally but throughout the English speaking world.

John Henry Skinner, known as "Harry" in the family, was born in Wisbech on 29th June 1860, second eldest of the four children of John Young Skinner, a printer and stationer. He later worked as a clerk for his uncle, William Stebbings, who was a prosperous timber merchant with a business in Station Yard, East Dereham (which was established in the mid-1860s) and who also owned considerable properties elsewhere. In 1872, William Stebbings & Co. were described as "Timber, deal, lath and slate merchants. Manufacturers of steam prepared mouldings and flooring". The company also had premises at South Gate Wharf, Lynn, for the importation of foreign timber. This was transported the twenty-eight miles to East Dereham by rail. Although the station at East Dereham was just opposite, the company had a spur line running directly into the premises.

John Henry Skinner had a good tutor in William Stebbings, and soon became an expert timber buyer, an accomplishment which was to stand him in good stead throughout his commercial life.

In 1875 William Stebbings & Co. were described simply as "Timber Merchants" and by 1883 described themselves as "English and foreign timber merchants and valuers". By this time their importation base had moved to Sutton Bridge in Lincolnshire.

John Henry Skinner and Elizabeth (Bessie) shortly after their marriage in 1883

In 1881, John H. Skinner was living at Oriel House, No. 65 Norwich Street, with his aunt and uncle, William and Emma Stebbings, together with Mary Skinner (Mr. and Mrs. Stebbings' sister-in-law), and a fourteen-year old maid, Edith Purple, was living in. William Stebbings was born at Forncett St. Peters in 1833, and his wife Emma was born at Upwell in 1838. (John Skinner's aunt, Emma Jane Stebbings, died on 12th April 1882 aged 44 years).

On 14th June 1883 John Skinner married Elizabeth Isaac at the Baptist Tabernacle at Great Yarmouth. Elizabeth, known as Bessie, was the school friend of John Skinner's sister Clara and the daughter of John Isaac, a wealthy joiner, builder, and timber merchant who owned timber mills at Middle Market Road and South Denes Road, Great Yarmouth. Clara Skinner had gone to work for John Isaac as housekeeper after leaving school.

OPEN FOR BUSINESS

In 1884 John Skinner began experiments in the production of plywood by hand, the first instance of plywood manufacture in the British Empire. He was also very interested in the hobby of fretwork and recognised the potential of plywood for this application. It meant that thin, but strong, sheets could be produced, often veneered with exotic species of wood which made economical use of expensive imported timber. At that time no fretwork machines and tools were manufactured in Britain, so he had to look further afield to Germany and America for supplies. He probably did not appreciate at the time that his interest in plywood and fretwork was to make his fortune and put Dereham on the map!

By 1887 John Skinner had entered into a partnership with Edwin Jackson Lyth and the business was described as "Timber merchants, dealers and converters of every description of English and foreign timber, also bent timber, dressed spokes, etc. Office, yard and mills, Railway Station". It is almost certain that Skinner and Lyth had taken on the timber business of William Stebbings & Co., which was no longer listed as timber merchants but as "Brick, tile, drainpipe, cement and granite merchants". William Stebbings was described as a valuer, and arbitration and commission agent, and appears to have retired from his timber merchants business.

THE EARLY FRETMACHINES

Prior to 1887, probably following his first experiments in the manufacture of plywood, John Skinner had set up another company, John Henry Skinner & Co., described as "Manufacturers and importers of fretwork materials". Tools and fretsaws were imported from Germany and America, and wood supplies came from Skinner & Lyth. The company was well established by 1887, as in that year J. H. Skinner & Co. published a catalogue of 32 pages plus cover, which cost 4d. and was printed by The East Norfolk Printing Co. at

Cover of J. H. Skinner's catalogue of 1887

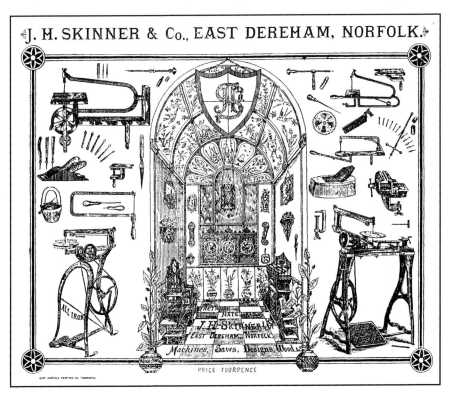

The Fleetwood

Yarmouth. In the editorial John Skinner wrote "we have found it necessary to extend our premises and increase our staff to meet the enlarged demand for our goods".

The catalogue illustrated a large range of fretwork designs, together with a good range of fretwork tools. All the treadle fretsaws and lathes were imported from America and some carried surprisingly high prices.

The top of the range machine was the "Fleetwood", which had a highly ornate stand, more befitting a Victorian drawing room than a workshop! This, complete with blower and boring attachment, cost £5.12.6, but could be purchased for £5.5.0 if a plain stand was required. A companion model mounted on a similarly ornate stand and nickel-plated, was the "Challenge" Scroll Saw (no attempt to hide its American origins here!) which, complete with a lathe attachment, cost £4.15.0. Another machine with a lathe attachment was the "Rival", at £3.3.0 complete with a set of turning chisels. This was made by the Seneca Manufacturing Co. at Seneca Falls, in Upper New York State. The approach of adding a lathe attachment to a fretsaw was very short-lived and appears to have been no more than a gimmick. Fretworkers soon found they were difficult to use and less stable than adding a fretsaw attachment to a lathe.

By far the most popular treadle fretsaws came from the manufacturers of the "Roger", a machine with simple but gracefully curved legs, In 1887 J. H. Skinner & Co. were importing the "New Roger", which was also advertised as the "Improved Roger". The price of only 16/6 explains why it was such a popular model. Even with a nickel-plated table and fitted with an emery wheel the cost of 20/- seems modest in comparison with the "Fleetwood" and "Challenge" machines. The "Cricket" fretsaw was of very similar but lighter construction to the "Roger" and without a blower or drilling attachment and sold

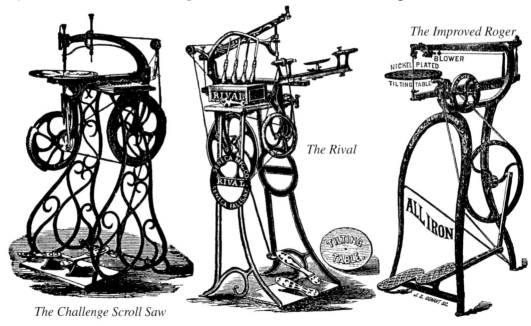

The Improved Roger

The Rival

The Challenge Scroll Saw

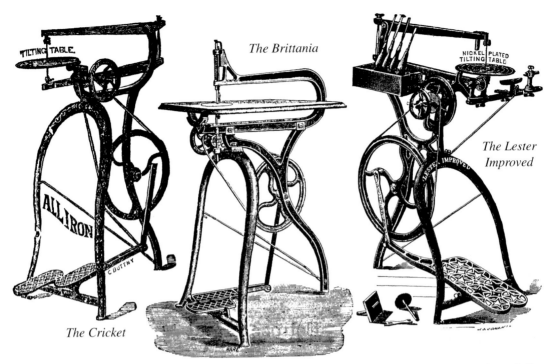

The Brittania

TILTING TABLE.

NICKEL PLATED
TILTING TABLE

The Lester
Improved

ALL IRON

The Cricket

for only 13/-. A similar basic design, with curved legs, was also used for the "Britannia", a much sturdier machine and one of the first to offer a saw with a true vertical stroke. It also had a very large table to offer support to large pieces of wood. Complete with saws, spanners and drills, this model cost £2.15.0. Also on the graceful curved leg stand came the "Lester Improved" model which offered a circular saw and lathe attachment as well as an emery wheel and drill and came complete for £2.7.6.

The Velocipede

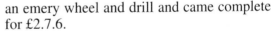

An unusual machine was the "No. 1 Velocipede Fretmachine" manufactured by W. F. & John Barnes of Rockford, Illinois. As its name suggests, this was driven by a pedal cycle arrangement instead of the usual treadle. The No. 1 machine, selling for £2.7.6, required the operator to provide his own seat but the later No. 2 model came complete with an iron seat similar to those fitted to early tractors!

Another unusual machine was the "Eclipse" hand machine. This was an adaptation of a hand frame which had a small table attached and was fixed to a table top by means of a clamp. The saw was operated by a handle under the table which was moved vertically up and down on a spindle, the upward movement was assisted by a powerful brass spiral spring. This sold for a modest 7/-.

The "Eclipse" series of hand machines took the design of table top models a little further. The No. 1333 model had a flywheel which was

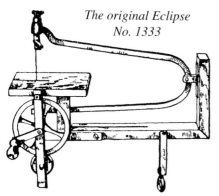

The original Eclipse No. 1333

cranked by hand to operate the saw movement and cost 9/6. Models 1081, 1082 and 1012, were all operated via a handle at the front of the machine which was simply moved up and down to operate the saw. These cost 4/6, 3/6 and 3/- respectively. The 1887 advertisement for these also advised that the three models could be operated by means of a cord looped to the foot!

The "Dexter A" machine made even further improvements on the requirement for the operator to stand on one leg whilst waving the other up and down! This was a table top model, based on the top frame and table of normal treadle fretsaw, which was clamped to a table top and the power was provided by a free standing treadle arrangement with long arms which, in turn, operated a small flywheel under the machine by means of a cord. This cost 25/-, whilst the "Dexter B" and "Dexter C" machines were more traditional models on iron stands with a treadle and sold at £2.15.0 and £3.5.0 respectively.

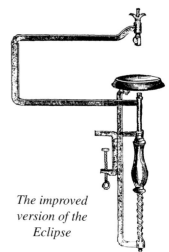

The improved version of the Eclipse

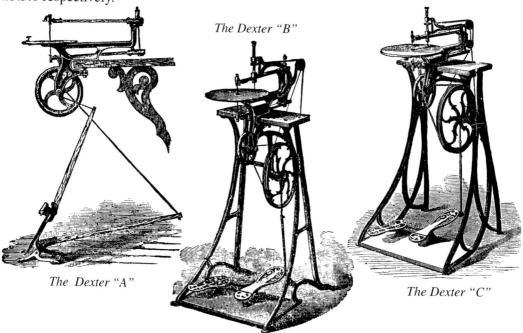

The Dexter "B"

The Dexter "A"

The Dexter "C"

In J. H. Skinner & Co.'s 1887 catalogue there were just two lathes, The "Companion" and the "Goodell". Both were of very similar construction, and both offered an optional fretsaw attachment. The "Goodell" was the superior machine having a better drill chuck than the "Companion" and with all bright parts nickel-plated and polished. The "Companion" sold for £1.15.0 (saw attachment 7/6 extra) and the "Goodell" cost £2.10.0 (saw attachment 10/- extra).

The Companion

The Goodell

The "Companion" lathe was destined to become a best seller and with minor modifications remained in production for over 60 years.

THE PHOTOGRAPHY BUSINESS DEVELOPS

Only one camera was offered in the 1887 catalogue, the "Eclipse" camera at 3/6 consisting of a polished mahogany sliding bellows 1/4 plate camera to photograph full size carte de visites, with focusing screen, dark slide, achromatic lens, brass fittings, developing and fixing chemicals, packet of dry plates and full instructions. For 7/6 the budding photographer could purchase a Complete Photographic Outfit which included the "Eclipse" camera together with printing

THE "ECLIPSE"

CAMERA SET,

3s. 6d.

Complete, consisting of a Polished Mahogany Sliding Bellows ¼-plate Camera to Photograph full-size Carte de Visites, with Focussing Screen, Dark Slide, Achromatic Lens, Brass Fittings, Developing and Fixing Solutions, Packet of Dry Plates, and full instructions, enabling any Amateur to take a good Photograph. Price 3s. 6d., or securely packed by Parcels Post, 4s.

frame, sensitised paper, gold toning bath, glass rods, cards for mounting and a hardwood folding tripod stand and focusing cloth. In the same advertisement J. H. Skinner also announced that they were starting to manufacture a "Guinea Camera Set" for which particulars would be sent on application.

Soon after this date advertisements began to appear in magazines, such as *The Practical Photographer, Work, The Practical Camera* and *The British Journal Photographic Almanac* for cameras, complete photographic outfits and photographic supplies.

In 1888, John William, the first of John and Bessie Skinner's six children was born. During the following years John William was joined by Conrad (later Rev. Conrad Skinner, Chaplain of Leys School, Cambridge), Reginald, Adelaide Frances, Cyril Frank and Dorothy Margaret.

On 14th May 1889 J. H. Skinner and E. J. Lyth, trading as J. H. Skinner & Co., made a patent application (No. 8054) relating to a rapid focusing device for camera bodies. So it appears that by 1889 Skinner and Lyth were in partnership, not only in the timber business, but also in the manufacturing and importation of photographic apparatus and fretwork materials. An advertisement of March 1890 in *Work* claimed that "J H S & Co. have now a large factory with accommodation for 100 workmen, which is used exclusively for the manufacture of photographic apparatus of every description from the cheapest to the most expensive".

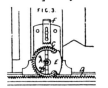

8054. Skinner, J. H., and **Lyth, E. J.,** [*trading as* J. H. Skinner & Co.]. May 14.

Cameras. — Relates to means for rapidly adjusting the camera for focussing p u r poses. Toothed wheels C, of larger size than the ordinary focussing-pinions, are keyed on the ends of an axis A, which can be turned by folding heads E, and which rotates in bearings B on the sides of the camera back frame. The wheels C gear into racks D fixed on the side of the baseboard, and can be locked at any point by the sliding bolts F.

The camera manufacturing factory was situated in Church Street, East Dereham (see inset in drawing opposite) and leased from Cook Wright Alexander, who had a drapery, millinery and tailoring business, together with a funeral services business in High Street. In the mid-1800s the building was occupied for many years by Edward Allen & Son, curriers and leather merchants. The building is now part of Aldiss Court, which is accessed from High Street. The three storey, flint and brick building was more recently used for storage by H. H. Aldiss, a large furniture and clothing retailer who purchased the business of C. W. Alexander in the late 1890s. When their large retail shop was purchased some years ago the premises were transformed into Aldiss Court, a small shopping precinct. As much of the old shop as possible, including the old camera factory, was incorporated into the Court. The building now accommodates shops and flats and the facade has been considerably altered, however much evidence of the original features can still be seen, although what is now the back was the front when used by John Skinner. The factory must have been approached from Church Street through what was known as White Lion Yard, a narrow lane adjacent to the White Lion pub. This was badly damaged in a Zeppelin raid in 1915 and now the site is occupied by the Inland Revenue Building. The side of the building once familiar to the 100 employees of J. H. Skinner & Co. may now only be approached through Old Pharmacy Yard, a modern name for the archway next to Dent's the Chemists. The prolific advertising campaign at this time, and the application for patents relating to camera mechanisms, suggests a manufacturing capability of reasonable size; yet to date no examples of the cameras attributable to J. H. Skinner & Co. have been discovered.

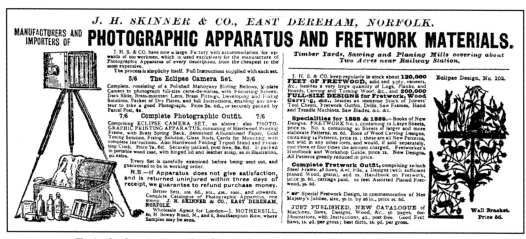

Typical advertisement for the products of J. H. Skinner & Co. of the 1890s

The works of J. H. Skinner & Co. in 1890 (the Camera Works in Church Street is inset in the circle)

Throughout 1889 and 1890 J. H. Skinner advertised their Eclipse camera at 3/6d. In the same advertisement the Stanley Complete Outfit was offered at 10/6, which was the same in all respects as the Eclipse outfit except for "folding tailboard, brass side bar and double dark slide in hardwood box with leather strap".

THE PARTNERSHIP IS DISSOLVED

The editorial in the 1890 catalogue announced *"To our customers. On April 19th of the present year (1890) the partnership existing between J. H. Skinner and E. J. Lyth, trading as J. H. Skinner & Co. was dissolved by mutual consent."*

"The stock was purchased by J. H. Skinner, the founder of the firm, who will continue the business under the unaltered style of J. H. Skinner & Co. There will thus be no change in the management."

An advertisement of 1890 advises customers that the partnership between J. H. Skinner and J. H. Lyth had been dissolved

The catalogue was accompanied with a leaflet making special offers with discounts of between 20% and 25% to clear "Cameras, stands, desks, &c". At the same time they offered 250,000 fretsaw patterns, 100,000 ft. of solid and three-ply fretwood, veneer etc. and 1000 gross fretsaws with a free book of fretsaw patterns with each order.

The 1890 catalogue of 36 pages, still costing only 4d., was printed litho by Page Bros. of Norwich and had a most interesting back cover (see previous page). This was illustrated by an engraving of the entire works of J. H. Skinner & Co. The buildings in the lower right corner are still there at the junction of Norwich Street and Station Yard but the Somerfield Superstore now occupies the rest of the site. Inset into the illustration is a picture of the building in Church Street, mentioned above, used by J. H. Skinner to manufacture photographic apparatus.

A further patent application of 31st July 1890 (No. 12001) for a turntable tripod mount in camera baseboards was made in the name of J. H. Skinner only, trading as J. H. Skinner & Co. Later in 1890 John Skinner appears to have entered into a partnership with Alfred Jermyn (later Sir Alfred Jermyn). However,

12,001. Skinner, J. H., [*trading as* J. H. Skinner & Co.]. July 31.

Cameras, stand attachments for. The baseboard C of the camera &c. is provided with flanges within which the turntable revolves. The latter is provided on its outer edge with a ring E from which a wedge-shaped portion has been cut. Into the broken part is fitted a wedge-shaped piece F, which can be moved inwards or outwards by a thumb-screw G, and thus serve to clamp the turntable in any position.

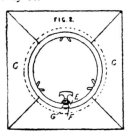

E. J. Lyth carried on the timber business on his own, an advertisement in a trade directory at the turn of the century informs the reader that Crane & Smith are now Timber Merchants in Station Yard - and the business was described as "Late E. J. Lyth" (Edwin Lyth died on 3rd November 1899, aged only 47 years). Advertisements for fretwork materials in the 1890s mentions that J. H. Skinner & Co. had timber yards, sawing and planing mills covering about two acres near the station. At this time employees were engaged mainly in making wood products which were packaged with tools and fretsaws imported from America and Germany.

By the end of 1890, advertisements by J. H. Skinner & Co. concentrated more on the fretwork side of the business than photographic equipment. However, in an 1891 year book J. H. Skinner's advertisement included the following statements:

- *J H S & Co. having all appliances, and a factory with accommodation for 100 workers, and a large staff of skilled London employees, call the attention of dealers to the fact that their best goods can successfully compete in style, quality and finish with the highest production of any London house, while the exceptional advantage enables them to sell the same article at a lower price.*

- *J H S & Co. give away no middle profits. They turn their own brasswork, make their own bellows, cut up the mahogany logs in their own saw mills, and season the wood themselves.*

John Skinner's assertion that London staff were superior no doubt did nothing to endear him to his Norfolk workers!

J. H. Skinner & Co.'s 1890 fretwork materials catalogue had just four pages devoted to photography and offered, in addition to the "Eclipse" camera, the Stanley (10/6), The "Half Guinea" (not surprisingly also priced at 10/6), the Moffat" (£1.1.0), the "Burke" (£1.1.0) and the "Marvel" (in three sizes, £1.1.0, £2.2.0, and £3.3.0). However, readers were invited to send for J. H. Skinner & Co.'s Photographic and Magic Lantern Catalogue which had "further Particulars and Prices of better Sets", with over 100 illustrations. This catalogue cost 2d., post free, and is a reasonable indication that the photography side of John Skinner's business was still thriving.

Contemporary advertisements claimed that J. H. Skinner & Co. had in stock about 120,000ft of fretwood, both solid and 3-ply, veneers, besides a large stock of logs, planks and boards, carving and turning woods. Over 200,000 full size designs for fretwork and turning together with an immense stock of joinery tool chests, fretwork outfits, drills, saw frames, hand and treadle machines and saw blades.

Advertisement from The British Journal Almanac of 1891

B Y 1895 John Skinner realised that instead of advertising in other magazines he should publish his own. This would give him the opportunity to publish articles on a variety of subjects, particularly fretwork, for which hobbyists would purchase the necessary materials and tools from his company. The fact that by purchasing the magazine readers would also be paying for his advertisements must also have appealed to him!

On 19th October 1895 the very first edition of *Hobbies*, described as a weekly journal for amateurs of both sexes, was launched. The magazine was called simply *"Hobbies"* when it was launched, it did not acquire the "Weekly" suffix officially until many years later, although it was known widely as *Hobbies Weekly* from its inception. The publication consisted of 24 pages printed throughout in black and priced at 1d. Popular belief was that it was produced in a redundant railway carriage which was parked next to William Stebbings' timber yard and that the fretwork business grew afterwards. But, as can be seen from the previous chapter, a substantial business had already been established.

The illustration on the back cover of J. H. Skinner & Co.'s 1890 Catalogue, mentioned in Chapter 1, does show what appears to be two railway carriages forming part of John Skinner's office. However, dispelling popular belief, the idea for *Hobbies Weekly* was not the idea of John Skinner but was actually mainly the brainchild of his younger brother, Frank Skinner. Whilst the idea for the publication was probably discussed in John Skinner's office, it is a romantic notion to conjure up mental pictures of editors wearing armbands and eyeshades, labouring away with quill pens in the cramped quarters of an old railway carriage! The imprint on the first edition stated the magazine had been printed and published at the Office of *Hobbies* at Bouverie House, Salisbury Square, London, EC. The sole advertising agents were John Haddon & Co., at the same address, and throughout the magazine requests were made for all correspondence to be addressed to The Editor of

PRESENTATION FRETWORK DESIGN WITH THIS NUMBER.

Hobbies
· A · Weekly · Journal ·
For Amateurs of Both Sexes.

No. 1.   VOL. I.   OCTOBER 19, 1895.   ONE PENNY.

Fretworking and Inlaying in Wood.
Photography for Amateurs.
Hobbies that Pay.
Stamps and Stamp Collecting.
The Magic Lantern, and how to make the Slides.
Bazaars and how to Decorate them.
An Electric Scarf Pin.
Cycling, Football, and Athletics.
A Fretwork Model of St. Paul's Cathedral.
Venetian Ribbon or Bent Iron Work.
Weekly Presentation Design.
Prize Competitions, Correspondence, Etc.

Hobbies, at the Bouverie House address. As the first editor was Frank Skinner, a journalist, who began his career on the staff of a Huntindonshire newspaper, but was then based in London, it does seems doubtful that the magazine was actually produced in a railway carriage in Dereham.

Publication of the first issue of *Hobbies Weekly* introduced the now familiar Hobbies logo. With only minor amendment over the years, and one short break, this logo was destined to be used for the next 100 years. The main alteration came very soon after its first appearance. A flourishing curl was added at the start of the flamboyant underline to replace the rather cut-off appearance of the original design.

FREE DESIGNS

The publication was accompanied with a free fretwork design for a midget photo frame. The trend of including a free design was to continue for the rest of the life of the journal, thereby offering the purchaser very good value. Annual subscribers to the weekly publication were rewarded with a free design for a fretwork model of St. Paul's Cathedral which would make up into a model 32 inches long, 21 inches wide and 22 inches high. The design was printed on six sheets and required 250 separate pieces to be cut. The front cover illustration shows the many diverse articles contained in the first issue, there were also advertisements for a number of suppliers of a wide range of hobby materials. One such advertiser was John Green, FRHS, who had moved his horticultural business in 1884 from Thorpe to a site, previously owned by James Moore, adjacent to Skinner's timber yard. John Green won many medals and diplomas at horticultural shows of distinction

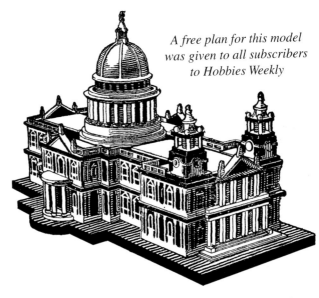

A free plan for this model was given to all subscribers to Hobbies Weekly

and was also honoured by the grant of a Royal Warrant, "By Appointment to Her Majesty Queen Alexandra". By the 1890s John Green was producing his own mail order catalogue.

The back cover advertisement of the first issue of *Hobbies Weekly* was for J. H. Skinner & Co.'s Annual Catalogue, price 6d including a presentation design for a model of Big Ben which stood 36 inches tall when completed. The advertisement claimed the catalogue was "New and Greatly Enlarged", (although the size was not specified), and that 10,000 copies had been printed.

Tucked away in the first issue was a small column dealing with the history of fretwork in which it was stated that "… a few indifferent Treadle Machines were sent over from America some twenty-five or thirty years ago. Since then rapid strides have been made, and it may safely be said that the Tools, Materials and Designs which are now produced in England are unequalled."

No doubt some of those "indifferent Treadle Machines" had been imported from America by J. H. Skinner & Co., but by the early 1890s a substantial engineering and foundry department had been established alongside the saw mills to manufacture fretsaws and fretwork tools. One model previously imported and sold by the firm was the "Roger", an elegant treadle machine with curved cast iron legs. It appears that Skinner copied the "Roger" as in an advertisement in Issue No. 4 of *Hobbies Weekly* dated November 9th 1895 J. H. Skinner claimed that all treadle fretsaws and lathes sold "were made by the company". Advertisements also claimed that they were the sole makers in Great Britain of steel hand frames, prices from 1/6 to 6/-. So it seems that John Skinner was adopting a policy of manufacturing own-brand products whenever possible, even if it meant copying someone else's ideas, rather than importing. Whether or not the copying was done under licence or by agreement is not certain, one thing which is certain is that many thousands of Roger machines were manufactured and sold over the next twelve years.

PRIZES GALORE!

Issue No. 1 also contained details of prize competitions which were being introduced. Prizes were offered for articles of fretwork, carving, designs, sketches, photographs, essays and numerous other subjects which would be introduced from time to time. The subject of the very first fretwork competition was the midget photographic frame, the design for which had been given free with the magazine. First prize was a treadle fretwork machine, with nickel plated tilting table, dust blower, and emery wheel. Second prize was a finely nickel plated and polished 14-inch hand fretsaw frame, and third prize was one gross of the best fretwork saw blades. The photographic frame had to be made up by the competitor and sent to Dereham for judging with a stamped label for return.

Winners of the first competition were announced in Issue No. 9. First prize was awarded to E. A. Grant, 7 Lovely Lane, Warrington and second prize to Edward C. Flann, 2 Meridian Terrace, Bishopston, Bristol. Because there were so many entries of a very high standard a total of six third prizes were awarded to Harry Beech, 18 Cherry Street, Wolverhampton; M. Stenning, 8 Fenton Street, Leeds; N. D. Brooks, 50 Argyle Road, Brighton; James W. Partridge, Lloyd's Bank Ltd., Alvechurch; Harold G. Neumegen, 34 Beaufort Street, Chelsea; and H. L. French (aged 11), Chancery Lane, Thrapston. The editor devoted two pages to comments about the entries, both criticism and praise, and mentioned names where appropriate.

Issue No. 10 contained details of the next competition, a much more ambitious project, a model of a horse-drawn coach "the Victoria", the plans for which were given free with that issue. Only two prizes were on offer, the second prize being the same treadle fretsaw machine which formed the first prize of the previous competition. But the first prize was

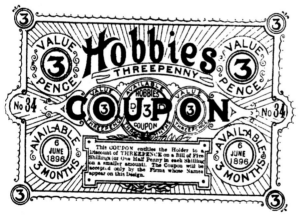

the magnificent "Imperial" treadle fretsaw with "superior tilting table for inlay work, vertical drilling attachment, and all modern improvements".

Another innovation which was introduced in Issue No. 3 was a discount coupon scheme. This consisted of a coupon printed on the weekly free supplement which was equal in value of up to threepence. These could be exchanged both with J. H. Skinner & Co. and with advertisers in *Hobbies Weekly* who had agreed to take them as part payment for goods supplied. Not more than 5% of the total cost could be paid by the coupons, for instance 5/- worth of goods required 1 coupon and 4/9 to be sent and 20/-

worth of goods required 4 coupons and 19/- to be sent. The coupons were valid for 3 months from date of issue and as the magazine cost only 1d represented quite a saving. In fact *Hobbies Weekly* claimed that for each 1d invested in purchasing the magazine the purchaser received 7d. worth of goods - the magazine worth 1d., a design worth 3d. and the coupon also worth 3d! And we thought that loyalty cards were a modern invention!

JOHN SKINNER STARTS A PUBLISHING COMPANY

One of the earliest publications sold by Hobbies Publishing Company in 1896

By the time the first issue of 1896 (No. 12) was published, John Skinner had decided that *Hobbies Weekly* was here to stay. An agreement was drawn up between John Henry Skinner, Frank Skinner and Thomas Absalom Clark "to acquire from 1st December 1895 the paper called *Hobbies*". On 4th February 1896 Hobbies Publishing Co. Ltd. was incorporated with capital of £3000 divided into 600 x £5 shares.

The shareholders were J. H. Skinner (100); Frank Skinner, journalist (100); Alfred Jermyn, warehouseman (40); T. A. Clark, coal merchant (40); Frank Clark, coal merchant (40); Walter Haddon, publisher (20); J. C. S. Brough, designer (20) and Fanny E. Smith, cashier (5). Directors were J. H. Skinner, Frank Skinner, Walter Haddon, Alfred Jermyn and T. A. Clark. The registered office was Bouverie House, Salisbury Square, London EC.

The division of Skinner's business interests was a wise move and was designed to limit the liability of what then became two separate companies. Hobbies Publishing Co. Ltd. became responsible for the publication of the weekly paper, *Hobbies*, also the publication of plans, handbooks and any other booklets, leaving the supply of materials and equipment in the hands of J. H. Skinner & Co.

Although articles in *Hobbies Weekly* were published on a wide range of crafts and hobbies, Skinner's advertisements concentrated mainly on selling fretwork kits, designs and tools. Particular pride was taken in the fact that seven prize medals had been gained by the firm in recent years: three gold at Tasmania in 1891 and 1892, one prize medal at Antwerp in 1894, and three at the Amsterdam International Exhibition in 1895.

J. H. Skinner & Co. Ltd. proudly proclaimed in their advertisement that it was the only firm in the United Kingdom to have obtained an award for fretwork designs or materials at any international exhibition.

An early "How-To-Do-It" book of 1896

In Issue No. 20 of February 29th 1896 the creation of Hobbies Supply Department was announced. This was set up to provide a service to the readers of *Hobbies Weekly*. Specimens of articles supplied by *Hobbies Weekly* advertisers were exhibited for examination in a showroom at Salisbury Square. At the same time a manager was appointed whose sole task was to answer queries from subscribers to *Hobbies Weekly,* and to acquire other items for them which J. H. Skinner & Co. did not stock. An innovative approach to customer satisfaction sadly lacking in this day and age!

It was obvious that by this time the fast growing circulation of *Hobbies Weekly* was bringing in considerable business to the East Dereham based supply company and so it was considered prudent to limit the liability of the directors of J. H. Skinner & Co. In April 1896 a Limited company was incorporated to trade under the name of J. H. Skinner & Co. Limited and was described as a "Photographic Apparatus, Fretwork Materials, Timber, Veneer, and General Fancy Goods Merchant". This company had seven listed shareholders: John Henry Skinner, East Dereham, Norfolk (Merchant); Alfred Jermyn, King's Lynn (Draper); Frank Skinner, 12 Paternoster Square, London (Journalist); James Carruthers Smith, 12 Paternoster Square (Designer); William Stebbings, East Dereham (Retired Timber Merchant); Hubert Alfred Jermyn, King's Lynn and Oliver Reynolds Jermyn, East Dereham (Norfolk Merchants Clerk).

The directors of J. H. Skinner & Co. Ltd. were J. H. Skinner (Chairman and Managing Director), Frank Skinner and Alfred Jermyn. The Registered Office was described as "The Factory, Dereham".

ON YOUR BIKE!

One of the most popular articles in *Hobbies Weekly* was the Cycling column. In Issue 25, cyclists were given advice about buying a bicycle. At that time a first class machine from one of the large manufacturers cost between £20 and £25, and readers were advised not to take their chances with firms who advertised cheap machines. It just so happend that a few pages further on the cycling readership could avail themselves of "an exceptional offer"! This announced that Hobbies had made an arrangement with a cycle manufacturer which allowed them to offer cycles at £11 each, instead of the more usual price of around £20 which was then current. Typically of the period, the advertisment was profusely worded compared with today's slick advertising, and the following is an extract from the advertisement:

THE HOBBIES' ROADSTER, £11.

This is a thoroughly useful Roadster, well-built and containing the very best materials. The wheels are 28 in. by $1\frac{3}{4}$in., and have Roadster hubs with tangent spokes and solid rims. The wheels are fitted with Dunlop tyres. The frame is made throughout of large-size weldless steel tubes, with narrow tread, dust-proof bracket, and $6\frac{1}{2}$-inch detachable cranks. It is fitted with rubber brake, mud guards, and

detachable foot rests. It is supplied with Lamplugh's hammock saddle, and will be fitted with rubber or rat-trap pedals as may be desired. It is geared to 60-inch, unless any other gear is ordered. The machine is enamelled black, and the handle bar, cranks, seat pillar, and other bright parts are highly nickel-plated. If preferred, the bicycle can be supplied as a light Roadster, without brake and guards, the weight then being 80 lbs. The price is £11, and the money must in all cases be sent with order. *Hobbies'* coupons will be accepted as part payment in accordance with the conditions explained on the Weekly Presentation Design.

HOBBIES' LADIES' BICYCLE, £11.

This is an admirable pattern for a ladies' machine, full room being allowed for the dress and for mounting, while the frame is specially strong and rigid. The size of the back wheel is 26 in., and of the front wheel 28 in. They have Roadster hubs with direct spokes and solid rims, and are fitted with Dunlop tyres. The frame is made throughout of best weldless steel tubing. There is a rubber brake to the front wheel, and the bicycle is fitted with rubber pedals, lady's hammock saddle, and patent leather chain dress guard with laced cord guard. The machine is enamelled black, with the bright parts handsomely nickel-plated. Price £11. The weight is about 34 lbs. Cash must in all cases be sent with order, and *Hobbies'* coupons will be accepted as part payment in accordance with the conditions laid down on the Weekly Presentation Supplement.

The article continued to claim that there would be a small delay in despatching orders due to the anticipated high demand and advised that orders should be sent "at once". The machines were guaranteed for one year, but this did not apply to accessories supplied by other manufacturers, such as tyres, saddles, etc.

Interestingly the bicycles were the first product to be sold under the *"Hobbies"* brand name, with the exception of the weekly paper, and were to herald the exciting changes which were to follow.

INNOVATION AND DEVELOPMENT

Issue No. 26 of April 11th marked the completion of Volume One. The only change to the cover during the first six months of publication was the addition of an illustration showing the free design for that week. In Issue 26 readers were notified that future numbers would have a coloured cover. The editor also said "that it had not been anticipated that *Hobbies Weekly* would attain so great and far reaching measure of popularity in so short a time". He added "the circulation of the paper already far exceeds the number which even in our most sanguine moments we hope to reach, and the circle of our readers is still widening every week with the most gratifying regularity." Despite the fact that the 26 issues had carried articles on a very wide range of hobbies, notice was also given that less space would be accorded to such subjects as fretwork and other distinctly indoor occupations which would be replaced by photography and other outdoor hobbies. Recognition was also made of the increasing number of lady readers and they were promised articles of interest to them would be published in future.

No hint was given that in issue No. 27 of 18th April, 1896, an announcement would be made that the offices of *Hobbies Weekly* had been removed to 12 Paternoster Square, London, EC where all correspondence should be sent in future. As mentioned in a previous paragraph, this was the address of Frank Skinner (a journalist) and James Carruthers Smith (a designer).

Issue No. 27 marked another milestone for the weekly publication. It was the first issue in which a half-tone reproduction of a photograph appeared. The previous 26 issues had all been illustrated with engravings. The illustration was a reproduction of a photograph, entitled "In Harbour - Morning", taken by L. West of Ravenshead, St. Helens which had won the First Prize of ten shillings in *Hobbies Weekly* March photographic competition. By a remarkable coincidence, the first half-tone reproduction of a photograph which was used in the local newspaper, "The Dereham & Fakenham Times", did not appear until eleven years later, and was a photograph of a fire which devastated Hobbies in 1907, which is dealt with in more detail in a later chapter.

The following issues were still mainly illustrated by means of engravings, but occasionally half-tone reproduction was used, mainly to illustrate winning photographic competition entries. It was, at that time, an expensive process but illustrates that the production of *Hobbies Weekly* employed the most up-to-date printing techniques of the time.

New articles were promised in the ensuing issues. Stamp collecting alternated with Coin Collecting. A series of articles entitled "The Mandolin and How to Play It" appeared in alternation with articles on Bookbinding. The popular Electrical articles had to alternate with Experimental Chemistry and old favourites such as Fretwork and Bent Iron Work were reduced in size so that more space could be devoted during the summer months to articles on Photography and Cycling. The ladies, who were promised "articles on novel kinds of fancy work" had to wait for issue 28 for their first article under the heading of "The Ladies' Workroom" which gave them detailed instructions of how to make "Two French Knickknacks"! These turned out to be a Parisian Photograph Holder and a Parisian Letter-Pocket.

Prize competitions were becoming more and more popular and valuable prizes were on offer of around one guinea for main competitions, such as Inlaying or Wood Carving and for writing an article for the publication, to ten shillings which was offered for the best photograph of the month. These prizes were the equivalent of between one and two week's pay for many of the readers of those days.

NEW PUBLICATION LAUNCHED

The circulation of *Hobbies Weekly* continued to grow and the Editor constantly boasted of receiving letters from readers in all parts of the world. The last issue of Volume 4 (No. 79 of April 10th, 1897) carried notice that a new weekly paper was soon to be published by Hobbies Publishing Co. Ltd. This was to be a sister publication to *Hobbies Weekly* entitled *"Live Stock Hobbies"*. The next few issues of *Hobbies Weekly* carried advertisements for a competition which was obviously dreamed up by a brilliant circulation manager! The total prize fund amounted to £50 and the top prize was to be awarded to the reader who increased the circulation of *Hobbies Weekly* the most. All competitors had to do was purchase not less than twelve extra copies of either issue No. 79, 80 or 81, and give them away free or sell them to friends and acquaintances! Careful note had to be made of all names and addresses who had been supplied with a copy of *Hobbies Weekly* and sent to The Editor. He would then judge whose efforts had been "most calculated to secure new readers for *Hobbies Weekly*"! It is not recorded by how many the circulation increased but it is a safe guess that the increased revenue created from such a creative idea must have far out weighed the investment of a paltry £50!

The first issue of *Live Stock Hobbies* was published on June 1st, 1897 and carried a similar inducement to increase circulation! However the top prize was halved to £5, but every competitor was promised a free subscription for three months, which in effect returned most if not all of the competitor's outlay. In those days many people kept a few chickens, rabbits, goats and other livestock and editorials in *Hobbies Weekly* forecast the same success for the new weekly paper as was enjoyed by their original publication.

The big event of 1897 was, of course, the Diamond Jubilee of Queen Victoria on 22nd June, and issue No. 89 for the following week carried an advertisement for a special design for a Victorian Commemoration Fretwork Wall Cabinet, price 6d. The cabinet was 30 inches tall, 16 inches wide and 7 inches deep and had been designed by "our special artist to celebrate the long reign of Her Most Gracious Majesty, Queen Victoria". Of course, Hobbies Supply Department could supply specially selected parcels of various suitable exotic woods and a bevelled mirror "at reasonable cost".

3   The Creation of a Legend

ON 16th June 1897, two historic Extraordinary General Meetings were held at The Factory, East Dereham. The meetings involved the directors and shareholders of Hobbies Publishing Company Ltd. and J. H. Skinner & Co. Ltd. Each had the same aim, to consider an amalgamation with a new company about to be incorporated under the name of "Hobbies Limited". This was confirmed at a subsequent Extraordinary Meeting held at the same place on 7th July 1897.

The new firm of Hobbies Ltd., a Joint Stock Company, was incorporated on 9th July 1897 with the registered office stated as 12 Paternoster Square, London. John Henry Skinner was appointed to act as liquidator with responsibility for the voluntary winding up of Hobbies Publishing Co. Ltd. and J. H. Skinner & Co. Ltd. He was also appointed as the first Managing Director of Hobbies Ltd. and Frank Skinner was appointed Editor in Chief of the Company's publications and London Manager of the Company for a minimum term of three years. Hobbies Ltd. was established with a nominal capital of £50,000, divided into 10,000 shares of £5 each.

The first shareholders who agreed to subscribe to the setting up of Hobbies Ltd. were:

John Henry Skinner, East Dereham, Timber Merchant;

Alfred Jermyn, King's Lynn, Draper;

Thomas Absalom Clark, Huntingdon, Merchant;

Frank Skinner, 12 Paternoster Square, Journalist;

James Carruthers Smith Brough, 12 Paternoster Square, Designer;

Oliver Reynolds Jermyn, King's Lynn, Merchant's Clerk;

Ernest Charles Thomas, East Dereham, Accountant.

The Articles of Association required that there should be a minimum of four directors

The Companies Registration Certificate showing the agreement to amalgamate J. H. Skinner & Co. Ltd. with Hobbies Publishing Co. Ltd. to form the new company, "Hobbies Limited"

and a maximum of seven, and each had to hold a minimum of 100 shares in his own right. The first four directors appointed were:

John Henry Skinner, Eckling Grange, Dereham, Chairman and Managing Director;

Frank Skinner, 19 Fairfield Road, Crouch End, London, London Manager of Hobbies Ltd. and Editor of *Hobbies*.

Alfred Jermyn, JP, Burleigh House, King's Lynn, Warehouseman;

Thomas Absalom Clark, Brooklyn House, Huntingdon, Merchant.

BARGAIN CLEARANCE OFFER

Most issues of *Hobbies Weekly* carried a column entitled "Hobbies Notes of the Week" where announcements of note were published, but no official announcement was made of the amalgamation and formation of the new company to the readers of *Hobbies Weekly*. It appears that the creation of the new firm was no more than a business convenience to combine under one company once again the business empire of John Skinner and his shareholders, and that no great changes were envisaged for their many customers. In issue No. 93 of 24th July 1897, the first clue appeared in an advert for Handbooks which had previously requested correspondence to be addressed to "Hobbies Publishing Co. Ltd." but now required orders to be sent to "Hobbies Ltd." at the same address. The first real notification came in an advertisement in issue No. 108 of 6th November 1897 for their new catalogue which had "just been published by Hobbies Ltd. with which is now incorporated J. H. Skinner & Co. Ltd". A design for the Eddystone Lighthouse, valued at 1/-, was given free to purchasers of the catalogue, which cost 6d. The advertisement also stated that the new catalogue offered fretwork goods at reduced prices and that all catalogues previously issued by J. H. Skinner & Co. were now cancelled.

NEW PRODUCTS LAUNCHED

Continuing to build on the enormous growth enjoyed by J. H. Skinner & Co., new products were soon to be offered by Hobbies Ltd. One of the first new machines offered by Hobbies Ltd. was released in November 1897. This was the "Hobbies" Hand Fretwork

Machine, which was designed to clamp to a table, the saw was operated by means of a crank wheel on the right hand side. The advertisement for the machine claimed that Hobbies had received innumerable letters from their customers, pointing out that none of the hand machines then on the market could be depended upon to produce good work, and so the "Hobbies" Hand Fretwork Machine had been introduced to cater for this demand. It will not escape the notice of the reader that many of the "hand machines then on the market" had been sold by J. H. Skinner & Co. Ltd.!

During the summer of 1897 Hobbies invested considerable capital in the engineering side of their business. In the autumn a steel hand fretsaw frame was the first product to be designed and made at East Dereham. Several of the machines used in its manufacture had to be specially constructed for the purpose and following prolonged experimentation and the introduction of ingenious labour-saving devices, Hobbies were able to turn out large numbers of steel hand fretsaw frames at reasonable cost compared to importing them from either America or Germany. At the time Hobbies was the only manufacturer of steel hand fretsaw frames in the United Kingdom.

In issue No. 112 of *Hobbies Weekly*, dated 4th December 1897, an announcement was made that the 24 page publication was to be enlarged to 32

The "HOBBIES" PATENT FRETSAW FRAME.

It may not be generally know that until quite recently all Fretsaw Frames used in this country had to be imported from either Germany or America. We are, in fact, the ONLY MAKERS IN THE UNITED KINGDOM of Steel Fretsaw Frames, and we have in our large Engineering Works, at Dereham, laid down extensive plant for the manufacture of these Frames. Several of the machines used had to be specially constructed for the purpose, but as the result of prolonged experiments and the adoption of ingenious labour-saving devices, we are now able to turn out large quantities of superior Frames at exceptionally low prices. The Frame, of which we give an illustration, is made of the very best British Steel, and the Clamps and the extremely simple device for tightening the Saw are constructed on entirely new principles, and are covered by Patents obtained by us. The saw can be fixed and tightened in far less time than was taken by the old screw tension arrangement. The Clamps are of Steel, whereas those in all the Foreign Frames are of malleable iron. PRICES—12in., 2/-; 14in., 2/3; 16in., 2/6; 18in., 2/9. Postage 3d. extra.

HOBBIES LIMITED, 12, Paternoster Square, London, E.O.

pages. The additional pages would allow for more articles and more advertisements, which had "shown a tendency to encroach upon the space devoted to reading matter" - now there was a novel approach! Also slipped into the paragraph was the casual announcement that advantage had been taken of the enlargement to incorporate *Live Stock Hobbies* into *Hobbies Weekly*. So, it appears, the extravagant claims in practically every issue of *Hobbies Weekly* that the sister journal was doing very well were "slight embellishments of the truth"!

As each issue of *Hobbies Weekly* was published so the list of subjects grew to impressive extremes of variance. Just a glance at the index to each volume would show that in addition to the usual hobbies of fretwork, photography, philately and metal work, the reader of *Hobbies Weekly* could expect to find diverse articles from "The Reasoning Power of Ants" and "Experiments with Flying Machines" to "Taxidermy". Every week a competition was run for the main subjects of fretwork and photography and issue No. 112 introduced two new regulars, Wood Carving and Bent Iron Work. What were, at the time, very substantial prizes, sometimes equating to three week's pay for a general labourer, no doubt played a part in the continuing popularity of the weekly publication. Issue 123 of 19th February 1898 carried claims that the circulation of *Hobbies Weekly* was growing at the rate of "several thousand copies a week"!

Hobbies Ltd. also continued to manufacture as many tools and machines as possible in their growing engineering works at Dereham; however they still had to import the actual

fretsaw blades. New products were constantly added to their range. In March 1898, the firm re-introduced cameras. The Hobbies "Crown" Hand Camera was a quarter-plate version and was offered at five shillings (hence the name). It would appear that these were manufactured specially for Hobbies and carried the firm's logo on the camera and carry case.

Hobbies Weekly also recognised the then new phenomena of workers being able to take holidays, and published many articles to advise their readers as to the best places to visit and how to spend their leisure time. For Easter 1998 *Hobbies Weekly* recommended trips of seven days to Rome for ten guineas, four days in Holland for five guineas, or a day trip to Calais for 15/- first class or 10/- third class. A return rail ticket from Dereham to London cost 8/-, more than half a week's pay for most workers.

DIVERSIFICATION

By this time Hobbies Ltd. were also manufacturing items other than fretwork tools and machines. The collapsible Cycle House, rain proof and dust proof, 6ft or 6ft 6ins long, 2ft 6ins wide, 4ft 8ins high at the front and 3ft high at the back. The cycle house, constructed of match boarding, cost one guinea for one machine, 26/- for two machines and 30/- for three machines. The Cycle Houses had first been manufactured by J. H. Skinner & Co., and each had the company name painted on the side as advertising. In May 1998 Hobbies Ltd. offered "A Comfortable Lawn Swing for Children and Adults - a pretty and most attractive article of garden furniture" for the princely sum of £2.10.0.

By the summer Hobbies Ltd. had introduced two more new cameras, Hobbies "Magazine" Hand Camera which had three double dark slides holding quarter plates so that six exposures could be made. This outfit, which came complete with four quarter plates, developer, fixing salts, sensitised paper and book of instructions, cost 5/9 and was described as "the cheapest magazine camera ever made". This was accompanied by the Hobbies "Postage Stamp" Camera, which would take six pictures on one quarter plate. Each camera had an extraordinary arrangement of six Achromatic lenses and "quick or slow exposures could be given". The price of the "Postage Stamp" was the same as for the "Magazine", at 5/9 and also came with a similar kit of chemicals, etc. In issue No. 135 of *Hobbies Weekly* a special photographic competition was announced, restricted to photographs taken by either Hobbies "Crown", "Postage Stamp" or "Magazine" cameras. First prize was a quarter-plate square camera and tripod, value £1.1.0. Second prize was a similar outfit but only valued at 10/6.

Also in the summer of 1898 Hobbies had spare capacity in their large plating and enamelling plant, which they aimed to fill by offering to re-plate bicycles "at small cost".

Come the autumn, Hobbies were once again pushing their fretwork tools, machines and kits to ensure that as many people as possible would be spending the long autumn and winter evenings making fretwork items. One advertisement advised the reader "Don't buy a cheap German Outfit at the Ironmongers" - even though J. H. Skinner & Co., had been importing the self same kits only a year or two previous!

Hobbies had a policy of maximising sales at any opportunity. A policy which, no doubt, played a significant part in building a substantial and successful company. One method employed was to make up parcels of surplus copies of *Hobbies Weekly* and send them out to large elementary schools for distribution to their pupils. The Headmaster of one of the largest boys' schools in London wrote to say that he had found a number of boys had been taking *Hobbies Weekly* regularly since such a distribution the previous year. The old adage "catch them young" springs to mind!

THE DEPOSIT COUPON SCHEME

Another scheme for extracting money from customers, even before they had made a purchase, was announced in October 1898 - the Hobbies Deposit Coupon Scheme. This was devised ostensibly for the benefit of regular customers to save them the trouble and expense of buying stamps or postal orders for small transactions. The Deposit Coupons were of the value of 1/- and made up into books. One contained eleven coupons and was sold for 10/6, and the other contained twenty-one coupons and was sold for £1. The maximum number which could be exchanged at any one transaction was five. This obviously saved the regular customer the cost of buying postal orders and gave him a useful five per cent discount. However, the scheme no doubt also made a significant contribution to Hobbies' bank account, and no doubt a significant number of coupons were mislaid and never were cashed.

Also in the autumn of 1898, Hobbies added another "off beat" product to their range, the Hobbies Shocking Coil. These were popular in late Victorian times to demonstrate the effects of electric current; it was also considered that mild electric shocks were medicinally beneficial. Manufactured at Dereham, the coils cost 7/10 and a powerful dry battery cost an additional 2/6.

4 *Expansion Gets Underway*

S INCE the creation of his original firm, John Skinner enjoyed considerable good fortune and his success in business had gone from strength to strength. Soon after the creation of Hobbies Ltd. a remarkable programme of expansion was embarked upon and a number of new products introduced. In issue No. 163 of *Hobbies Weekly*, dated 26th November 1898, it was announced that the second Hobbies Supply Stores was to be opened in London, at 166 Aldersgate Street. This opened for business during the first week of December, and one of the attractions for Londoners was a demonstration by a fretworker, cutting and assembling items live in the window! It was also promised that on a weekly basis, commencing the first Tuesday in January, a member of the *Hobbies Weekly* editorial team would be present to give advice or just chat to any readers who might like to drop in.

PRAISE FROM THE PRESS

By this time the weekly circulation of *Hobbies Weekly* was 50,000 copies and the same issue also boasted that the circulation was increasing "at a phenomenal rate, by from one to two thousand every week"! This claim was no doubt precipitated by the recent publication of an article in the *Eastern Daily Press,* in their series on "The Industries of Norfolk", which heaped praise upon the Dereham based business. Ever modest, *Hobbies Weekly* referred to the article, which they said was too large to quote in full, but they thought that their readers would be interested in reading a "few extracts" - which, in reality, amounted to most of the article! However, the article contained some historically interesting facts and figures, and the extract which appeared in *Hobbies Weekly,* is reproduced below.

"It is probably no exaggeration to say that customers of Hobbies are to be found in every town and nearly every village in the country, while orders arrive daily from the remotest corners of the world. Some idea of the enormous and far-reaching character of the business transacted by the company may be gained from the statement that it is no unusual statement for more than a thousand letters to be received in a single morning at the Dereham and London offices of the company. Every week Hobbies Weekly enters more than 50,000 homes, not merely in Great Britain but in Australia, Canada, Africa, and even such remote countries as Chitral and Afghanistan. Hobbies may, indeed, be said to be following the flag, and it will be in all probability not long remain unknown in Omdurman and the Bhar-el-Ghazal.

"It is, however, chiefly in the description of our Dereham Works that our own readers will probably be most interested, and we therefore reproduce a few paragraphs dealing with the various Departments. The Company's New Saw Mills immediately face the entrance to the Dereham Railway Station, and are imposing buildings fitted with the most modern Machinery. They were erected to take the place of Mills which, although only completed three or four years ago, were found altogether inadequate to meet the requirements of the Company's rapidly growing trade. One of the most interesting features in the Saw Mills is a costly Vertical Band Saw. It was, we believe, the first machine of its kind laid down in this country, and anyone with even a slight knowledge of sawing machinery will be able to judge of its capacity when we say that it will cut boards from logs at the phenomenal rate of 1,000 feet per hour. Another exceedingly useful and very ingenious Machine is employed for the purpose of giving a smooth and glossy surface to the boards as they come from the saw. Fed through rollers, the boards pass over an accurately adjusted knife, the edge of which is ground to the sharpness of a razor, a perfectly

smooth and, indeed, almost a polished surface being given to the boards at the rate of about 500 feet an hour. At the time this machine was laid down it was, with the exception of two belonging to Her Majesty's Government, the only one of the kind in Great Britain.

"Hobbies Ltd. are also very large importers of Foreign Fancy Woods, and at the time of our visit it was estimated that their present stock of Fretwood—one of the most important branches of the Company's business—exceeded one million feet. An idea of the quantities purchased may be gathered from the fact that the mere carriage from Liverpool to Dereham of one lot of Satin Walnut recently received came to nearly £200, and this related to but a single purchase of only one description of wood.

"But the Company has other premises of an even more imposing character. On entering the Dereham Station, indeed, from the direction of Lynn or Norwich the name of Hobbies is the most conspicuous feature on either side of the line. In addition to the Saw Mills and Timber Yard, there is on the right side of the line a magnificent range of buildings containing some twelve thousand square feet of floor space. Here are the head offices of the Company, and here, too, are store rooms and packing rooms where the many hundreds of orders daily received by post are duly attended to. In this building there are also various descriptions of woodworking machinery devoted to the manufacture of Fretwork Materials and Photographic Apparatus, and behind it are the immense stores of fancy woods for the use of Fretworkers, and another building in which wood is rapidly dried by currents of hot air set in motion by specially constructed machinery.

"On the opposite side of the railway is another large building which constitutes the Engineering Department of the Company. In the Engineering Works attention is largely directed to the manufacture of Fretwork Machines and Fretwork Hand Saw Frames. Until Hobbies Ltd. founded this Department nine-tenths of the Fretwork Machines and every one of the Hand Saw Frames sold in this country were imported from either Germany or America. The Company proved the possibility of beating our foreign competitors both in respect of price and quality, and as a reward for the enterprise they displayed they are rapidly securing the monopoly in Great Britain of this class of trade. The machinery which is already laid down and working to its fullest capacity, is able to turn out 250 complete treadle machines and 1,000 hand frames each week. There are also a number of subsidiary departments in connection with the Engineering Works. There is, for example, a branch for the manufacture of small electrical goods, such as shocking coils, motors, plating outfits, etc. This is in the charge of a very able electrician, and promises to develop into a very important department. There is also a very complete electro-plating plant, and all kinds of nickel and silver plating is done on the premises. The Works, indeed, on both sides of the railway, possess many features of quite exceptional interest.

"It is a business conducted on absolutely new lines, and without any rival in the country. With such a business covering so wide a field, what limit can be placed upon its possible development?"

Advertisement for Hobbies' 1898 annual catalogue

31

EASY TERMS AND JOB OPPORTUNITIES

During 1898 Hobbies experimented in the sale of treadle fretwork machines on a weekly payments system. This proved to be very successful and several hundred machines were sold by this method.

Early in 1899, prompted by letters from customers, this method of selling was extended to include costly photographic equipment.

In issue 177, 4th March 1899, of *Hobbies Weekly* an advertisement invited readers to apply for the post of an "Expert Fretworker to publicly work a treadle machine at the Hobbies Supply Stores at 166 Aldersgate Street, London". From among the many applications, one received from a Dublin reader was printed in the following issue - the letter is reproduced above.

No doubt all the staff, from the Editor down to the office boy, would have been made to feel very insecure by the appointment of a gentleman with such varied accomplishments, and the application was politely turned down!

By March 1899 further expansion was under consideration. Requests for Stores had been received from a number of places, including Newcastle, Cardiff, Manchester, Liverpool, and Sheffield. In order to gauge where the most demand was, readers were asked to send in a postcard to nominate their choice of location.

PHOTOGRAPHY RE-INTRODUCED

In the early 1890s the photography business of J. H. Skinner & Co. was substantial, but it had been eclipsed by the growth of the fretwork business to the extent that it seems to have almost disappeared altogether. The Church Street factory certainly was only in use for a comparatively short time, probably four years at the most. However, in March 1898, Hobbies had reintroduced cameras to their range, as described in the previous chapter, and in March 1899 the firm expanded the range by introducing their No. 1 Hand Camera at 5/9, and later Hobbies offered 5/- each for about a dozen negatives which had been taken with the camera which "suited their needs". What these were was not divulged, but presumably they were required for advertising purposes.

In June the patented Hobbies No. 2 Hand Camera was introduced at 10/6 and represented significant improvement over the No. 1 model, being able to hold six 1/4 plates which were held in metal sheaths and moved into position automatically after each exposure.

A month later saw the unveiling of the Hobbies No. 4 model at £1.10.6. What happened to No. 3? - This was called the Hobbies "Quick Firer" which did not seem to carry a model number but was similar to the No. 2 except that it carried twelve 1/4 plates. Later in the year a Hobbies Film Camera and Outfit was introduced at 5/-.

HORTICULTURAL BUSINESS ACQUIRED

For many years John Green had operated a horticultural nursery adjacent to the Hobbies Ltd. site and had frequently advertised his plants and seeds in *Hobbies Weekly*. On 1st July 1899 his business was amalgamated with Hobbies Ltd. The business was purchased by John Skinner, acting as agent for Hobbies Ltd., for £4,000 of which £2,000 was paid in cash and the balance of £2,000 was paid by the allotment of 320 ordinary shares of £5 each (then valued at £6.5.0 each). Hobbies Ltd. acquired the premises, plant and machinery, carts, office furniture, trees, plants and seeds and undertook to carry out all contracts and engagements which had previously been entered into by John Green. The purchase also included the goodwill, the use of the name "The Norfolk Nursery and Seed Establishment" and the right to use the words "late John Green" in advertisements to indicate that the business was to be carried on as a continuation of the previous ownership and was described as Hobbies' Horticultural Department. Soon after the amalgamation an autumn and spring catalogue was published, for 1d., advertising hyacinths, tulips, crocuses, narcissi and other Dutch bulbs, strawberry plants, roses, shrubs, climbers, fruit trees, bushes, raspberry canes, seakale, asparagus and rhubarb.

THIRD SUPPLY STORE

In late August 1899, Hobbies announced that their third Supply Stores was about to open at 9 Lime Street, Liverpool, at the junction of Lime Street and Lord Nelson Street.

Issue No. 207 of *Hobbies Weekly,* dated September 30th 1899 was accompanied by an eight page Hobbies Horticultural Supplement, which was the first of what was to become a regular addition to the popular weekly publication.

QUACK CURES AND NEW TECHNOLOGY

Just to further illustrate the wide range of articles published in *Hobbies Weekly,* an earlier issue included an article on how to cure toothache, earache and baldness. The one for baldness would quickly ascertain who your friends really were! "Take the yolk of an egg, a wine-glassful of cod-liver oil, and a wine-glassful of expressed juice of onion. These are very thoroughly mixed, and the lotion rubbed into the roots of the hair once or twice a week"! One of the cures for toothache was equally obnoxious: "If the offending member has a hole in it, you may try the insertion of any of the following that takes your fancy: A small piece of camphor, a bit of opium, a plug of cottonwool wetted with chloroform, spirit of camphor, tincture of myrrh, Eau de Cologne, turpentine, laudanum. (the last is probably best)". One has to hope that no-one was unfortunate enough to suffer from baldness and toothache at the same time!

By the end of 1899 Hobbies were capitalising on what was then a luxury product, mainly available to the upper classes - electricity. For many weeks *Hobbies Weekly* had published the occasional article on generating electricity and the construction of accumulators and in the autumn brought out a small catalogue devoted to "Electrical Novelties". This included Electric Lighting Sets, Bell Outfits, Electric Scarf Pins, Burglar Alarms, Plating Outfits, Telephones, Telegraphic Sets, Electric Alarm Clocks, etc.

In the first week of December 1899 Hobbies' fourth Supply Store opened in Glasgow, at 326 and 328 Argyle Street. Issue No. 216, of Hobbies dated December 2nd 1899 appealed for fretwork articles made by Glaswegians to display in the "very large and fine window of the store". The same article also claimed that Hobbies had "an almost unlimited amount of window space" at their Liverpool Supply Store where they would be happy to stage a similar display.

The famous "A1"

MORE MACHINES INTRODUCED

Also in December 1899, Hobbies claimed that for every fret machine sold a few years previously they now sold at least a hundred and whilst they had been satisfied with constructing machines based on the American imports, Hobbies had seen the faults of these machines and had begun to invent machines of their

The Royal Hobbies

own including the "Royal Hobbies", the "Imperial" and the "Hobbies A1".

The Imperial

The last issue of *Hobbies Weekly* in 1899 advertised that a new 120 page Hobbies Garden Guide was just about ready for despatch at the price of 6d., or 9d. post free. However, as a special offer for a limited period, Hobbies were offering the Guide free on receipt of 3d. to cover the cost of postage. A somewhat conflicting statement! The same issue promised new articles for the new year which included "How to Build Model Yachts", written by a naval architect who was "engaged in one of the principle ship-building yards on the Clyde", and "Watch Repairing for Amateurs".

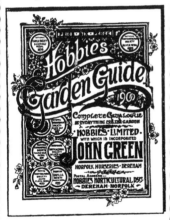

Throughout the South African War *Hobbies Weekly* continued to supply designs for patriotic items such as photograph frames and "Tommy Atkins" pipe racks. The "Ladies' Workroom" section provided details for making cholera belts, comforters and mufflers.

EXPANSION CONTINUES

In early June, 1900, Hobbies opened their fifth Supply Stores, and the third in the capital, at 153 Bishopsgate Street Without, London. All the fixtures for the new shop, were manufactured in Hobbies' factory at Dereham. But Birmingham customers of Hobbies had to wait until the end of the year before the sixth Hobbies Supply Store was created at 75 High Street, at the entrance to the New Arcade. This opened in the

"Tommy Atkins" Pipe Rack

first week of December 1900 and featured a practical display of fretworking in the window, a trait which had become established at the opening of earlier Supply Stores.

Hobbies' fifth Supply Store at 153 Bishopgate Street Without, London

In September Hobbies launched their eighteenth Annual Catalogue of 112 pages, printed by Page Bros. of Norwich.

Also illustrated in the pages of Hobbies 1900 Annual Catalogue was the Model Steam Engine No. 2 and details of the Superior Model Steam Boat No. 2. These appear to have been German imports and had been introduced a year or two before the end of the century. Later, steam powered engines and boats were to play a significant part in the history of Hobbies.

William Stebbings, who had started John Henry Skinner on his illustrious business career, died on 30th June 1900, aged 67 years, and was buried in Dereham Cemetery on 5th July 1900 in the same grave as his wife, Emma Jane.

During 1900 Hobbies Horticultural Department gained a number of awards at various national shows and in 1901 a number of new articles were promised for *Hobbies Weekly* including "Astronomy as a Hobby".

GOOD NEWS FOR SHAREHOLDERS

The third Annual Meeting of Shareholders was held at the end of 1900 and the Chairman, John Skinner, presented a glowing report of the year's trading activities. Despite the effects of the war (the Boer War) and the inevitable increase in raw material costs, he said that all departments had shown a good

trading result, especially the retail stores and the growing sales of *Hobbies Weekly* had made a significant contribution to the profitability of the company. Considerable investment had been made in the engineering works and foundry and a saw mill had been purchased in Athlone, Ireland, for which the company had paid cash. Overall the company had made £4,699.13.5 profit but the company deemed it prudent to restrict the share dividend to 5% to leave sufficient capital to allow further expansion. Therefore the amount available for distribution by way of dividend for the year was declared to be £2,331.12.5.

Model Steam Engine, No. 2.

No. 2.—This is a beautifully finished Engine on stand, with brass boiler and brass cylinder, fitted with safety valve and regulator.

Post Free, 3/9.

Superior Model Steam Boat, No. 2.

This is a large and very superior screw action Steamboat, painted white, with a solid brass boiler, and fitted with safety valve. It travels through the water at a great speed.

Post Free, 5/6.

A Journey at Christmas

THE dominating news story of early 1901 was that of the death of Queen Victoria on 22nd January, ending her illustrious reign of 63 years. Never one to miss an opportunity to capitalise on an event (no doubt under the auspices of paying their respects) the black edged issue of *Hobbies Weekly* dated February 9th, included a free design for an "In Memorium" frame with the promise that at a later date a "large and imposing Victoria Memorial design" would be published. And, of course, the very next issue included a design for a "Long Live The King" decorative shield to commemorate the accession of King Edward VII.

The Board of Directors at that time had increased to six. In addition to the original four directors two more had been appointed: Herbert Jewson of Norwich Road, Dereham, an engineer; and Matthew Hallwright, 215 Hagley Road, Birmingham, a surgeon.

On 22nd November 1901 a Prospectus was published inviting the public to subscribe to the balance of 3,383 Preference shares of £5 each. A small paragraph in *Hobbies Weekly* a week or two before had invited readers to apply early thereby giving them an advantage over the general public. This appears to be the first time that Hobbies' shares were offered publicly and the firm was obviously endeavouring to raise additional capital to help finance their expansion plans. The Prospectus showed the turnover in the years to 30th June as being in 1899, £37,883.3.9; in 1900 £45,646.3.5; and in 1901 £54,219.19.9. Profits in the same years were 1899 £2895.15.8, in 1900 £3,778.15.3 and in 1901 £4,545.1.10 - a remarkable increase in profits of 57% over the period. The average weekly circulation of *Hobbies Weekly* was 65,000 copies in 1901.

SUCCESS—FOLLOWED BY MORE SUCCESS

During the year Hobbies' Horticultural Department continued to gain successes in various shows. At the meeting of the National Dahlia Union, held at Westminster Aquarium, they obtained the distinctive award of the Society's Large Gold Medal. Hobbies' exhibit was the only one to obtain this highest award. At the great Floral Fête at Shrewsbury they were awarded a Large Gold Medal for their collection of begonias, gloxinias and dahlias.

A prize-winning display at the National Sweet Pea Show at Westminster Aquarium, 1901

At the National Sweet Pea Show at the Westminster Aquarium they were awarded the Society's Gold Medal. At the meeting of the Royal Horticultural Society, held at Westminster Drill Hall, Hobbies' exhibit of dahlias was awarded

Hobbies' prize-winning display at the National Dahlia Union meeting in 1901 - taken with "one of Hobbies' cheap stand cameras"

the Flora Gilt Medal. At the Boston Dahlia Show they were awarded the Silver Medal for the best trade exhibit, and the highest award of a Gold Medal was awarded to Hobbies for their huge collection of chrysanthemums, roses and dahlias at the October meeting of the National Chrysanthemum Society. In addition the Horticultural Department obtained numerous First Class Certificates

and Awards of Merit in various shows.

At the end of 1901 an article in *Hobbies Weekly* informed the reader that in spite of the war and the prolonged depression caused by the war the circulation of the weekly paper had increased to record levels. The volume of business transacted at the retail stores had taxed to the full the production capacity at the company's factory at Dereham. And so, for a while, Hobbies capitalised on their investment in their six retail outlets and concentrated on

Commemorative Diploma awarded to Hobbies Ltd. for their huge collection of cactus dahlias at the Glasgow International Exhibition, 1901

introducing an increasing number of machines, tools and designs to their range. The output from the Horticultural department, under John Green's guidance, was also ever-growing and 40 extra acres of land was acquired and additional seed warehouses and packing rooms had to be erected. The Engineering Department also patented an iron framed greenhouse which, they claimed, was "practically indestructible". Ten of these new greenhouses were erected in Hobbies' Nurseries for inspection by prospective purchasers. The 1902 Horticultural Department annual catalogue ran to 144 pages and included a bewildering range of just about every plant imaginable.

An impressive collection of gold and silver medals awarded to Hobbies' Horticultural Department - photograph published in the 1902 annual catalogue

FUNDS RAISED FOR FURTHER GROWTH

On 30th April 1902 a further issue of 2,894 Cumulative 6% Preference Shares of £5 each were offered at par. The list of subscribing shareholders included Obadiah Pursey, who owned a men's outfitting business in High Street, Dereham (now Dereham DIY); John Skinner on behalf of his six children: John William Skinner, Conrad Arthur Skinner, Adelaide Frances Skinner, Reginald Stebbings Skinner, Dorothy Margaret Skinner and Cyril Frank Skinner; also John Skinner and George Jewson acting as executors of the late William Stebbings.

In mid-December 1902 the seventh Hobbies Supplies Stores was opened in Leeds, at 15 County Arcade - an imposing building, described by Hobbies as "large and commodious premises".

The new Leeds store - opened in 1902

At the end of 1902 an agreement was made to combine the timber merchants businesses at Athlone, Ireland, which had been purchased in 1900, with that at 317 Holloway Road, London, which had been acquired earlier, into a separate business. Hobbies New Timber Co. was incorporated on the 20th of October 1902, with nominal capital of £26,000 divided into 6,000 preference shares of £1 each and 20,000 ordinary shares of £1 each. The shareholders at the time of incorporation were:

Alfred Jermyn, King's Lynn, Warehouseman (800 Preference, 200 Ordinary);

John Henry Skinner, Dereham, Timber Merchant (200 Preference, 200 Ordinary);

John Green, Dereham, Horticulturist (300 Preference, 200 Ordinary);

Frank Skinner, 12 Paternoster Square, London, Journalist (1 Ordinary);

Joe Kaye, Harrogate, Timber Merchant (200 Ordinary);

Herbert Jewson, Dereham, Engineer (200 Preference, 200 Ordinary);

Oliver Reynolds Jermyn, Athlone, Timber Merchant (800 Preference, 200 Ordinary);

William English Smith, Athlone, Ireland, Timber Merchant, (345 Preference);

Sydney Cozens-Hardy and Frank Jewson, Castle Chambers, Norwich, Solicitors, (500 Preference);

Hobbies Ltd. 12 Paternoster Square, London, Manufacturers of Fretwork Materials, (6,000 Ordinary).

Directors appointed were:

John Henry Skinner, Dereham; Alfred Jermyn, Burleigh House, King's Lynn; Oliver Reynolds Jermyn, Athlone, Ireland.

DISTANT SHORES BECKON

During 1903, John Henry Skinner, who had been the brains and the driving force behind the successful growth of the various businesses since before 1887, decided to part company with Hobbies to emigrate to Durban, South Africa, to start a veneer and plywood manufacturing business.

As mentioned in Chapter 1, John Skinner had a long standing interest in the production of plywood and he recognised there were far more uses for the product than just for fretwork. He recognised that to convert timber to plywood was making the most economic use of the wood and he perceived that the varied commercial uses in which the thin sheets of plywood could be utilised were endless. No doubt there was scope to exploit the opportunities available following the end of the Boer War, he would also be close to the sources of exotic timber which had previously been imported into Britain at high cost.

By the end of December 1903, John Skinner had resigned his directorships with both Hobbies Ltd. and Hobbies New Timber Co. and his brother Frank took over as Managing Director of Hobbies.

A FAREWELL CONCERT

John Skinner was held in such high esteem by his workforce that on Wednesday, 16th December, the employees of the firm arranged a Smoking Concert at the Freemasons' Hall in Norwich Street, Dereham, in order that they could make their farewells to a much loved employer.

The chairman was Mr. A. G. Smith, the manager of the fretwork department of Hobbies, who had known John Skinner since their early teens. He was supported by Mr. J. H. Skinner, Mr. Frank Skinner, Mr. John Green (managing director of the horticultural department), Mr. J. C. S. Brough (secretary), Mr. E. C. Thomas (assistant secretary and brother-in-law of John Skinner), Mr. O. R. Jermyn (managing director of Hobbies New Timber Co. Ltd.), Mr. R. J. E. Green, Mr. E. C. A. Green, Mr. C. E. Hughes, Mr. C. Smith, Mr. W. H. Page, Mr. C. D. Marr, Mr. H. C. Wier, and Messrs Geo. Brett, T. Cranmer, G. H. Goodchild, H. G. Himson, O. Pursey and others. Approximately 180 of the employees from the Dereham works were present.

The proceedings opened with the National Anthem, after which various toasts were proposed and songs were sung by Messrs. G. Cooper, R. Cooper, H. G. Himson, R. J. Oliver, and C. Smith. The chairman read telegrams of good wishes from the managers of Hobbies' retail shops and in proposing "The Health of Mr. Skinner" he said that when Mr. Skinner had decided to take up an extensive business in South Africa he expressed the desire to meet all the employees for the purpose of saying farewell to them. He continued with a glowing account of how Mr. Skinner had created a firm which had grown from very small beginnings to one which was then known world-wide.

In his reply, Mr. Skinner thanked the chairman for all the kind remarks made about him and he paid tribute to the loyalty of the employees. He said that it had been his privilege to take the lead of the firm, but if it had not been for able colleagues, good foremen and men who believed in doing a good day's work for a good day's pay, the company would not be in its present flourishing condition.

He continued to say that he felt that he had to offer each worker some small remembrance of himself, and this took the form of a framed portrait photograph. He also expressed the wish that each department should arrange for their photographs to be taken which could be formed into a group, and he assured the company that the picture would have a very prominent place in his new home.

PRESENTATIONS AND SONGS

The chairman, on behalf of the employees, then presented to Mr. Skinner an illuminated address in album form. The album, which was supplied by Geo. Coleby, a well known Dereham printer and stationer, was very handsomely decorated and bound in red morocco leather and bearing an exquisitely engraved monogram "J.H.S." in heavy silver gilt, with gilt pierced corners.

The address contained inside read as follows:

"We, the employees of Hobbies Limited, beg you to accept this address as an expression of the esteem and confidence in which you have been held by us during the years you have acted as managing director of the company. It has all along been our pleasure to work harmoniously under you, and sincere regret at your departure for South Africa, and consequent severance of your personal connection with the active business of the firm, is shared by every department.

We offer you, with your wife and family, our best wishes for health and prosperity in the land to which you are going, and it is our earnest hope that your new home may be blessed with all the happiness which has surrounded the old home at Dereham."

Then followed a list of the names of all the employees of Hobbies Ltd., both in the manufacturing and retail departments in Dereham and the various retail outlets around the country.

The expenses of the Smoking Concert were not deducted from the amount subscribed towards the address, but were paid for by H. J. Jewson, J. C. S. Brough, E. C. Thomas, Miss F. E. Smith, C. E. Hughes, E. C. A. Green and C. Smith.

Mr. Frank Skinner made a short speech, and introduced himself to the employees at Dereham and assured everyone of his intentions to try to carry on his duties as managing director in the same earnest manner that his brother had done. He also informed them that he would soon be coming to Dereham to reside.

A song had been specially written for the occasion by Mr. R. J. Oliver and was sung by him during the evening:

I greet you fellow workers,
I am glad to meet you here,
To bid farewell to those who've seemed
So far and yet so near.
We will wish them the safest voyage
To Africa's foreign strand,
And hope one day to welcome them back
To their own dear native land.

Chorus:

Then, hurrah, my boys; the sails they are set;
May the winds blow soft and fair.
They're bound for distant Durban,
And in a few weeks they'll be there.
'Tis hard to part with those that we love,
And the one that has taken the lead,
But we're here tonight, both one and all,
To wish our old boss "God speed".

There are some of us who remember,
In days long years ago,
When the firm of J. H. Skinner,
Was only a tiny show,
But by one man's prudence and forethought,
It has grown to great renown,
And has made the town of Dereham,
Known almost the whole world round.

The firm is now called "Hobbies",
And many new faces are here;
But the face and form of our old boss,
Will ever to some be dear.
And though more new faces may still arrive,
And the firm turn upside down,
We shall remember the face of him
Who raised "Hobbies" in Dereham town.

Before I bring this song to a close,
I'll wish our old boss long life.
Long life and happiness to him,
His children, and his good wife,
And if we meet them here no more,
To shake them by the hand,
I trust that we shall meet some day
In that promised better land.

DEPARTURE AT CHRISTMAS

This was the third farewell meeting that John Skinner had attended during the third week of December; a week later, on Christmas Day 1903, John Henry Skinner, his wife, Bessie, and their six children, left Dereham station by saloon carriage on the 5.40 train. Many of the employees and heads of various departments assembled at the station to see them off. The Wesleyan Church, of which Mr. Skinner was circuit steward and trustee (and a liberal supporter) was also strongly represented. Also present were several prominent Dereham businessmen including, H. H. Aldiss, R. Armstrong, C. Cory, T. Cranmer, R. Oldham, and Rev. A. Kirk. Mr. Skinner shook hands with those present and wished success to all and then the train left amid a chorus of good wishes.

The Skinner family embarked on board the "Briton" on Boxing Day and sailed for their new life in South Africa where John Skinner established a new firm, Plywoods (South Africa) Ltd. at Prince Alfred Street in Durban, and became the first Managing Director.

Earlier, plywood was manufactured by hand, a slow laborious and expensive operation. In South Africa, John Skinner applied his skills to adapting suitable machinery and evolved a method of making plywood by machine which was both precision made and cheap. Huge tree trunks were cut into logs of approximately 7 feet in length and boiled in hot steam in huge concrete containers for between 12 and 18 hours. This softened the wood, especially the knots, and dispersed any resin in the wood. The logs were then placed on the veneering machines, similar to large lathes, and as they were spun a knife moved into the log cutting veneers 1/16 inch thick which were peeled off at the rate of 300 feet per minute. These were cut roughly to size then dried and rolled on another huge machine with 700 rollers, each 12 feet long, and two miles of steam pipes. After drying the sheets were cut to size ready for the gluing process. This was an automatic process, an unglued sheet of veneer was placed on the machine, another was fed in, glued both sides and with the grain at 90° to the first sheet, a third sheet of veneer was laid on top, with the grain in the same direction as the first then rolled and a pile of finished sheets were placed in a hydraulic press. After sanding and cutting to size the sheets were ready for sale.

Skinner produced two grades, ordinary quality for interior use, and waterproof for exterior use. The later was made of such a high standard that it easily met the American standard for plywood to be used in the construction of aeroplane wings. This required the glue to withstand boiling in water for 24 hours, followed by baking at 212°F for a further 24 hours, or soaking in water for 14 days. Soon John Skinner's products were being exported all over the world and revolutionised the furniture industry and house construction, and plywood was soon utilised in all sorts of other applications.

At Hobbies New Timber Co. Frank Skinner was appointed in place of John Skinner and Herbert Jewson was appointed as a new director.

MORE PRODUCTS—MORE SHOPS

Hobbies Ltd. continued a policy of introducing more items to their range and in their 128 page 1904 Annual Catalogue the Hobbies Patent Norfolk Fretsaw was announced. This was very elegant but sturdily built and designed to saw wood up to 1 inch thick. The machine also allowed for speed control utilising a system of small and large pulleys, and there was also the facility to allow the machine to be worked by power instead of treadle. However, it was over five times more expensive than the popular A1 machine, being priced at £5.7.6 as against £1.1.0. The Norfolk Machine was later joined by the very similar Suffolk version but neither were kept in production for very long due, no doubt, to their high cost.

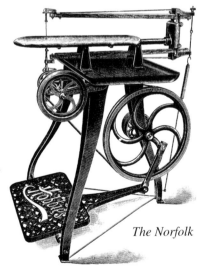

The Norfolk

At the end of 1904, Hobbies, as a continuation of their expansion policy, opened another shop at 10a Piccadilly, Manchester, which was destined to become one of the most successful of their chain of retail outlets. This was followed during subsequent years by retail shops being opened at 214 West Street, Sheffield; 25 Bernard Street Southampton; and 68 London Road, Brighton - although it wasn't until 1938 that the final retail shop was opened at 13 Prospect Street, Hull. Many agents had also been appointed in major towns and cities throughout the country and abroad, especially throughout what was then the "British Empire", including Canada, Australia, New Zealand, and India.

6   *Fire! Fire!*

IN 1907 Hobbies was to suffer a major disaster. On Thursday 28th February, two employees were working late. At approximately 7 pm one, Dennis Brooks, accidentally upset a can of heating oil which was ignited by a nearby naked flame. On the floor above, a clerk named Walker was making up pay books for the following day. He heard a crackling noise and went out to investigate only to find that the flames had already spread to the top floor. He leapt through the flames, leaving his coat and paysheets to their fate. The efforts

The charred beams show the severity of the blaze

Still damping down on the following day

Employees and managers survey the damage

of the two men to extinguish the flames were in vain and the building was soon well ablaze. The top floor was used to store paint and oils and the cans exploded in the heat allowing their contents to pour down in streams to feed the flames.

The Dereham Fire Brigade was summoned. But their horse-drawn Shand Mason steam fire engine was no match for the inferno which faced them on their arrival. The Fire Brigade also had a covered horse-drawn van which was used to convey the firemen and coal for the steamer to the fire. The horses for both were provided by the King's Arms Hotel in the Market

The rear of the engineering department pictured on Friday 29th February 1907

Place (now replaced by Woolworth's) and were normally used to pull the hotel's fly, or carriage, to and from the railway station to collect patrons who travelled to and from the town by rail. Sometimes the horses were harnessed to the fly, sometimes they were running loose on a nearby meadow, so turn-out times were significantly longer than we are used to nowadays. The Fire Brigade also had an escape ladder but this had to be trundled to the fire by hand.

SEVERE DAMAGE

By the time the Fire Brigade arrived the fire had spread to over a quarter of an acre and was threatening the railway station and Crane & Smith's woodyard, which stood on railway property. All they could hope to do was contain the fire and protect adjacent cottages, which had been emptied of their contents, as best they could. The G.E.R. Railway fire engine was summoned by telegraph from Norwich to protect railway property. Parts of Crane & Smith's buildings, stables and warehouse were lost, but horses, including those belonging to the railway, were saved. The firemen were there until well after midnight.

The devastation in the engineering department

A new gas engine, which had been installed by Hobbies at a cost of £1,200 only the previous week to drive the shaft and belt system in the factory, was destroyed. The damage to Hobbies' property amounted to £25,000 and 150 men were put out of work. Practically all of the machinery was lost or severely damaged and could not be easily replaced as it was unique, having been built by Hobbies, and most of the wooden patterns, or moulds, from which the castings were made were destroyed in the fire.

The Dereham Fire Brigade of 1907 who had to tackle the inferno

NEW STYLE MACHINE

Also lost in the fire were moulds used to manufacture popular fret machines like the "Roger", which had been in production since 1895 when J. H. Skinner & Co. Ltd. copied the American made machine.

By the Autumn of 1907 Hobbies were back in production with "an entirely new pattern treadle fretsaw" the construction of which, they claimed, "differs considerably from any machine we have previously offered". This was "The Briton", and the advertisement went on to contradict the headline mentioned above by saying: "The Briton is designed after the pattern of our well-known Roger Machine which has been literally sold by thousands in the last two or three years. All the parts of the machines are interchangeable…".

The main casting of "The Britain" appears to be identical to that of "The Roger", the main visible differences being a different pattern flywheel, the words "The Britain" replacing the words "The Roger" at the top of the gracefully curved legs, and the Hobbies logo being incorporated into the treadle casting. The price of 15/6 in 1907 was 6d. less than that charged in 1895 for "The Roger".

The popular Roger machine re-incarnated as The Briton after the blaze

7

Re-organisation and Disruption

DURING 1907 Hobbies Ltd. appointed leading ironmongers in main towns and cities as official agents. Fifty two agents were appointed initially, in addition another Supply Store was created in Leeds, at 21 and 22 Vicar Lane, and a Horticultural Depot was established at 17 Broad Street Place, London. The first agent abroad was also appointed. It is not certain whether Hobbies' founder, John Skinner, had any influence in the appointment, but Messrs. James Wyllie and Sons, 62 Strand Street, Cape Town, Cape Colony, were appointed agents for Hobbies Ltd. in South Africa.

Company records show that by the end of 1907 Frank Skinner had resigned from the boards of both Hobbies Ltd. and Hobbies New Timber Co. and a new director, Richard Jewson, St. Clements, Norwich, timber merchant, was appointed to both boards. The Manager of Hobbies New Timber Co. was O. R. Jermyn, and the Secretary of the company was Ernest Charles Thomas, Dereham, (Assistant Secretary of Hobbies Ltd.). Edward C. A. Green (son of John Green) was appointed Company Secretary and Manager of Hobbies Ltd.

RIVAL PAYS HOBBIES SUBSTANTIAL DAMAGES

What is not made clear in the company records is why two directors and two other employees left to set up a rival firm called Home Handicrafts Ltd. It appears that before they left they had taken a filing cabinet containing records of the names and addresses of 80,000 Hobbies' customers and had sent them free copies of a rival paper similar to *Hobbies Weekly* and solicited orders. In the issue of *Hobbies Weekly* of 28th December 1907 appears a statement made to the customers of Hobbies which stated that on 6th December 1907 Hobbies had obtained an injunction from His Lordship Mr. Justice Pickford in the King's Bench Division of the High Court of Justice, restraining Handicrafts Ltd. and Frank Skinner, James Carruthers Smith Brough, Fred Clark and Winnie Smith (late employees of Hobbies Ltd.) from making use of card indexes, lists, order envelopes, and documents containing the names and addresses of Hobbies' customers to whom they had sent circulars and magazines and were forbidden to solicit orders or business from Hobbies' customers. Hobbies were awarded £1,500 damages and costs.

Hobbies were alerted to the situation when they received hundreds of letters from customers who either expressed surprise or complained that their names and addresses had got into the hands of people with whom they had not had contact. Hobbies' policy of regarding their customers as "one big happy family" certainly diverted a potential business disaster on this occasion.

From this point relations between the two firms were somewhat acrimonious and Hobbies and Handicrafts Ltd. were to cross swords again at a later date.

NEW BOARD TAKES OVER

So, at the beginning of 1908, for the first time the board of directors of Hobbies Ltd. did not include a member of the founding Skinner family, and consisted of:

Alfred Jermyn (Chairman), Burleigh House, King's Lynn, Warehouseman;

Matthew Hallwright, Birmingham, Surgeon;
John Green, Norwich Street, Dereham,
　　Nurseryman;
Herbert Jewson, Norwich Road, Dereham,
　　Engineer;
Richard Jewson, Norwich, Timber Merchant;
Edward C. A. Green, Norwich Road, Dereham,
　　was the Company Secretary.

RE-ORGANISATION COMMENCES

Following his appointment to the board of directors, Mr. Richard Jewson set about the task of reorganising the company. One of the first changes occurred on 14th January 1909, when the Registered Office of Hobbies Ltd. was transferred from 12 Paternoster Square to Norwich Road, East Dereham.

As part of the reorganisation strategy Hobbies New Timber Co. ceased trading on 10th October 1912. Also by this time, following a world tour by Richard Jewson, nine official Hobbies Ltd. agents were established in Canada and another in Prahran, Victoria, Australia, as well as "all the principal Hardware Stores in Melbourne, Adelaide, Sydney, Calcutta, Bombay and all large cities".

*The new chairman of Hobbies,
Alfred Jermyn*

One of the biggest innovations in fretwork for many years was introduced to Hobbies at this time by an Italian priest, Monsignor Antonini, who had developed the "antofret" system of fretwork. This consists of bevel cutting into a single piece of wood, so that when the cut-out piece was pushed up it had an overlaid and in some cases a carved appearance. Several articles were to be published in following issues of *Hobbies Weekly* devoted to items utilising the antofret system, and many fretworkers became expert at using this new development of the hobby.

Matthew Hallwright, director

In 1913, John Green retired from active management, but retained his directorship, and went to live in Kew so that he could enjoy the amenities of the gardens which he loved so much.

Also in 1913, following the Annual General Meeting of Hobbies Ltd., Richard Jewson was paid

*John Green, director and founder of
Hobbies' Horticultural Department*

£500 as special remuneration for exceptional services rendered to the Company in connection with the reorganisation of its affairs during a period of six years ending 30th June 1913. Unfortunately the outbreak of the First World War, or the European War as it was known initially, was to scupper the best laid plans of any organisation.

HOBBIES COPES WITH WAR

War with Germany was declared at 11pm on Tuesday 4th August 1914. The following day the 5th Battalion Norfolk Regiment was mobilised. At lunch time the Dereham detachment of the 2nd East Anglian Field Ambulance Brigade assembled in the Market Place and left from the station following tearful farewells from their wives and families. By the evening 800 men were billeted in F. & G. Smith's maltings in Norwich Road which were commandeered for the purpose. The top floor of Hobbies' warehouse on the east side of the railway was also commandeered to provide quarters for the officers.

Men of the 5th Battalion Norfolk Regiment ready to leave Dereham Station on 9th August 1914

On the 9th August the 5th Battalion Norfolk Regiment left Dereham railway station for its War Station at Colchester, taking with them the many horses which had been commandeered from local businesses. A number of the men had been employed by Hobbies and their departure in such a short time-scale obviously had a considerable effect on production.

By early September it was realised that the war was not to be as "short, glorious and victorious" as some politicians were forecasting. Some were predicting "It will all be over by Christmas", but The Secretary of State for War, Lord Kitchener, was forecasting the war would last three years. Consequently a recruitment campaign was commenced and locally a reserve battalion of the 5th Norfolk Regiment was raised. Lloyd George had managed to whip up a general feeling of patriotism and commitment to the war and many young men answered the call and volunteered for service. The minimum age then was nineteen, but many under that age managed to slip through the checks. The average labourer's wage at the time was 15/- per week, and the Army pay of 1/- per day with all food and clothing found, combined with a sense of adventure, formed an attractive draw for many local young men, thereby depleting Hobbies' workforce even further.

More and more women began to take the places of soldiers who had gone off to war. Initially women began to appear behind shop counters and in offices more frequently than before the war. Gradually women were taken on by industry to perform work hitherto

In 1914 Hobbies were contracted to make school desks - this is one of the models, the "Special"

considered too heavy for females. Hobbies was no exception and soon female labour was employed in all departments including the engineering works and the foundry. The expertise of Hobbies' engineers was soon to be instrumental in obtaining a number of Ministry contracts for the production of munitions.

Issue No. 1,000 of *Hobbies Weekly* was published on 12th December 1914 and contained a special contribution by Mr. Gillie Potter, a well-known broadcaster of the time. Even for Hobbies, who published articles of an extremely wide interest range, this was "something different". Potter's contribution was a short play, entitled *"The Secret Code"*, the tale of The Great War in two scenes. Complete instructions were given for staging and playing *"The Secret Code"* as well as hints on successful make-up and staging the play in aid of the National Relief Fund, of which the Prince of Wales was President. The play brought a letter from the Secretary of the fund thanking the Editor for his efforts.

Fiction was also tried in *Hobbies Weekly* at another time, but did not prove popular and was dropped - as were articles about hobbies of special interest to the fairer sex. One of the most popular series of articles were contributed by F. T. Bidlake, the doyen of cyclists and cycling journalists at that time. Also similarly enjoyed at the time were articles by G. H. Westwood on making model aeroplanes - *Hobbies Weekly* was always at the forefront in advances in technology and soon involved their readership. Electricity and radio are just two further subjects that were exploited for the benefit and enjoyment of amateur hobbyists.

Ever mindful of the welfare of their readers, in June 1915 *Hobbies Weekly* published a Coupon for £250 worth of Insurance which had been arranged with General Accident. The terms of the insurance were somewhat limited as it only covered those aged between 14 and 65 years who were fatally injured or killed in an accident whilst travelling on a passenger train. The author was unsuccessful in trying to ascertain how many claims had been received under the offer!

ZEPPELIN RAID ON DEREHAM

On the evening of Wednesday, 8th September 1915, Dereham suffered a bomb raid by a German Zeppelin. Over seventy high explosive and incendiary bombs were dropped on the town and surrounding area. The worst of the damage occurred in the vicinity of Market Place and Church Street. Altogether two local men, James Taylor and Harry Patterson, and three City of London Yeomanry soldiers were killed. The Germans claimed in a communiqué after the raid that they had attacked "great factories near Norwich" and they had observed "heavy explosions and numerous fires", and had been "heavily fired at by hostile batteries".

Townsfolk survey the bomb damage in Church Street where the photographic studio of Herbert Cave, the grocery store of Richard Hamerton, and the White Lion pub were wrecked

Press censorship prevented mention of the Zeppelin raid at the time in local newspapers other than the following brief statement: *"TWO SUDDEN DEATHS. It is with deep regret that we record the sudden death of Mr. James Taylor of High Street, East Dereham, which took place on Wednesday evening. He was present at a property sale on Wednesday afternoon, and purchased some cottages. His end was so sudden as to be absolutely painless.*

Mr. Taylor, who was 61 years of age, has been in business in Dereham for about 24 years. He is survived by his wife and two sons.

The greatest sympathy of the townspeople goes to Mrs. Taylor in her bereavement. Her husband was highly respected by everyone. He took a keen interest in the town affairs, and was a keen member of the Voluntary Training Corps and a Special Constable.

The death occurred on Wednesday of Mr. Harry Patterson, watchmaker and jeweller, of High Street. He was the only son of Mr. Wm. Patterson of Commercial Road, and was about 41 years of age. He was a married man but had no family". No mention was made of the deaths of the three soldiers.

After the war a report of the Zeppelin raid was published, thanks to the "partial lifting of press censorship". A "full" account of the raid was given and the main damage seemed to have centred around the Market Place, and contemporary photographs would appear to support this. The "heavy explosions" reported by the Germans after the raid could have been the oil and cartridge store of Bradley's, the ironmongers in the Market Place, which took a direct hit. The firing of the maroons to summon the fire brigade, after which the Zeppelin quickly departed, accounted for the "hostile batteries". However, the Germans also claimed they had hit "great factories near

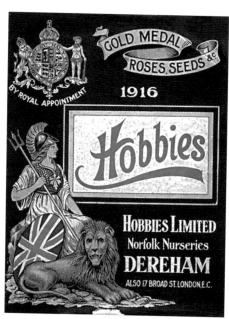

Hobbies' Horticultural Department catalogue of 1916

Norwich". This was always thought to have been an "exaggeration of the truth". But in the December 18th issue of *Hobbies Weekly* the introductory paragraph of "The Editor's Note Book" stated: *"As many of our readers are already aware, a considerable portion of the Engineering Works of Hobbies Ltd. has been destroyed by fire.*

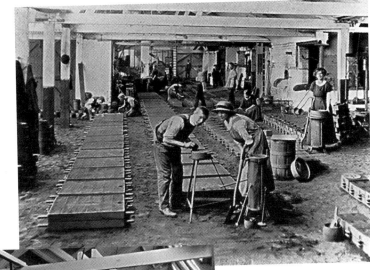

Above: Female labour working in the foundry, 1917

Left: The power press shop, 1917, showing the complicated system of shafting and belts used to drive the machinery

Below: Another view of the power press shop, illustrating the involvement of female labour

This is extremely unfortunate at this period of the year, when the Christmas trade is just getting into its stride, but seeing that good stocks are always kept in the Supply Department which has escaped unscathed, fretworkers may rest assured that most of their wants will be supplied." It is therefore reasonable to suspect that the fire damage at Hobbies was the result of an incendiary bomb dropped

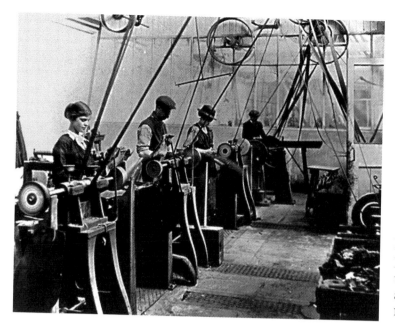

Employees hard at work in Hobbies' grinding shop in 1917

from the Zeppelin, either during the raid or as the Zeppelin left for home. No reports of the fire were ever made in the local press at or near the time, nor at a later date. Because Hobbies were heavily engaged in producing munitions no doubt any reports would have been suppressed by the War Ministry, even after the war had finished.

PATRIOTISM BOOSTS PROFITS

The weekly publication of *Hobbies Weekly* continued seemingly unaffected by the War, except that due to severe paper shortages the page content had to be reduced from 32 pages to 20 pages in 1917, and later to 16 pages. Most issues contained instructions and plans for making items connected with the War. Very popular were wooden toys, including a siege gun, a motor ambulance, a coastal defence gun, a 4.5 Howitzer and a tank. Fretworkers were urged to make several models for sale as cheap toys. The design for the siege gun, for instance, included the following encouragement: "A working gun is a good selling line at all times, but during the war and for some time after there will be some difficulty in entirely supplying the demand for a cheap working gun. The most popular line is that selling retail at $6\frac{1}{2}$d., and produced at 3s. 3d. per dozen. Such a toy is the siege gun which should be packed in a neat box, with a supply of ammunition, this being short lengths of 3/16 in. doweling."

Fretworkers had always been encouraged in *Hobbies Weekly* to sell their products, more so in wartime when they were to find a ready market as most of the

View of the assembling benches in 1917

Assembling fretmachines in 1917

cheap tinplate toys of the time were imported from Germany. Obviously this also had the desired roll-on effect on Hobbies' profit margins who probably sold more plans, fretsaws and parcels of wood than before the war!

Also very popular were the seemingly unending range of patriotic picture frames, mirrors, and overmantels, all depicting some aspect of the war, particular regiments, or royalty. In the autumn of 1915 a "Great Jig-saw Puzzle Competition" was announced with 60 cash prizes totalling £100, again on a war theme. Of course, Hobbies could supply a specially prepared competition parcel containing the two pictures required, "Hill 60" and "The Sinking of the Blucher", two panels of fretwood and two boxes to contain the puzzles, when completed, for 2/6.

Stories of fretworkers then occupied in the various services were also frequently published, and often there was a special section for servicemen in fretwork competitions. In the January 6th, 1917, *Hobbies* was proud to publish an account of bravery by Second-Lieut. G. R. Mason, who had been a clerk in Hobbies Head Office at Dereham and used to live in Quebec Road, Dereham. When war broke out he had joined the Gloucester Regiment and went out to France where he had "some thrilling experiences"!

One of these experiences involved bringing up machine guns under intense enemy fire and organising machine gun defence of each objective as gained and holding the positions when won. Lieut. Mason lost three fingers of his right hand in the engagement and for his courage and initiative was awarded the honour of the Military Cross.

Operating a lathe in the engineering department in 1917

View of the sawmills in 1917

Many pages of *Hobbies Weekly* were devoted to gardening tips and readers were encouraged to crop any vacant plot of land, as some food stuffs were in short supply. Each article was accompanied by a special offer from Hobbies' Horticultural Supply Department! U-boats were sinking merchant ships so there were no imports of bananas, oranges or tinned fruit and meat. There were no fancy cakes at the bakeries, just "standard" loaves. Often barley, rye or even potato flour was added to the wheat flour to make it go further, but the result was often a grey and heavy loaf. Most of the good quality leather was requisitioned by the army, so boots and shoes were made of inferior leather, and many fathers had to learn the art of cobbling, assisted by helpful articles in *Hobbies Weekly*. Supplies of paraffin and oil were sporadic and often townspeople had to queue for supplies at Bradley's in the Market Place, or Cordle's in High Street. However, priority was given to keeping factories in production, especially those like Hobbies who were engaged in munitions work.

NEW TOYS INTRODUCED

During the war Hobbies also managed to introduce new ranges of toys to satisfy the home market now that imports had dried up. One very popular range was

A 1917 view of the woodworking department

the "Klipit" construction outfits which consisted of different lengths of prepared square section wood which were joined together by means of simple metal clips. Five different outfits were made ranging in price from 3/6 to 21/- and each outfit contained a number of metal parts so that mechanical models could be made. As well as details of construction projects included in each outfit, Hobbies did not miss the opportunity of publishing in their weekly paper designs for other "Klipit" models based on the war theme, such as battleships and a Red Cross wagon.

Operating planing machines in the woodwork department, 1917

Another popular toy which was introduced was the "Stripwork Construction Kit", which in some ways was similar in concept to the "Klipit" range of kits except that more involvement by the hobbyist was required. Each kit contained a bundle of prepared stripwood and a small range of tools which included a small tenon saw, hammer, tiny plane, drills and sanding block to enable the stripwood to be made into a large range of useful as well as decorative items.

Due to the shortage of workers, the Horticultural Department was closed down towards the end of the war. Those who had been employed there were transferred to other more important duties in the engineering or woodwork departments. These included S. R. Rudd who joined Hobbies as a clerk in the Horticultural Department on 1st January 1901. He subsequently rose to become head clerk of the Horticultural Department, responsible for dealing with the mail

Staff leaving off for breakfast, 1917

Left: The "Klipit" construction kit introduced in 1917

Right: The Suffolk fretmachine launched in 1917

Lower left: Advertisement for the newly introduced "Stripwork" outfits

THE SILENT TEACHER

Hobbies

TRAINS THE HAND AND EYE.

STRIPWORK

BRITISH-MADE OUTFITS.

OUR OWN MANUFACTURE.

No. 3 Outfit
7/6
Post Free
8/3

LISTS FREE ON APPLICATION. WRITE TO-DAY.

HOBBIES LIMITED, DEREHAM,
AND FROM ALL BRANCHES AND AGENTS.

order business from an office which used to be situated opposite the Memorial Hall, in Norwich Street. However, in 1919, John Green's eldest son, Reginald, purchased back the Horticultural Department and acquired land off Norwich Road to continue the family's association with horticulture in Dereham. Green's Nurseries, for a time, continued supplying the large range of seeds and plants which had been supplied before the War. Later, when the firm had passed to Reginald's son, John, they concentrated mainly on trees, shrubs and roses, but as transport costs increased the firm began to concentrate on soft fruits, such as blackcurrants, raspberries and strawberries, which were mainly sold for canning to companies such as Huntley & Palmer.

After the war the board of directors consisted of:

Alfred Jermyn, Burleigh House, King's Lynn, "Gentleman of No Occupation";

Richard Jewson, The Old House, Old Catton, Norwich, Timber Merchant;

Matthew Hallwright, Birmingham, Surgeon;

Herbert Jewson, Norwich Road, Dereham, Engineer;

John Green, 42 West Park Road, Kew Gardens, London, "Gentleman of No Occupation";

Edward Charles Annison Green, The Shrublands, Norwich Street, Dereham (now Dereham Labour Club), Manager and Secretary. (Newly appointed to the board).

Herbert Jewson, director

8

Heydays and Great Days

FOLLOWING the Great War it took the country some time to recover from its effects. It was hardly surprising that an intense anti-German feeling prevailed for many years after the war, in fact until well into the 30s. Hobbies capitalised on this loathing by using every opportunity to advertise the fact that their products were "British Made by British Workmen". For some time the Union Jack was incorporated as often as possible in advertising in their annual Catalogues and, of course, in *Hobbies Weekly*.

In 1920, Mr. William F. Chambers was appointed Editor of *Hobbies Weekly* and became responsible for providing interest, knowledge and enthusiasm for amateur craftsmen all over the world. He had begun his journalistic career with the Yarmouth Independent and was injured at Monchy during the First World War. William Chambers was also Publicity Manager and charged with managing an annual budget for advertising in the home market and the export market which ran into many thousands of pounds.

A view of the engineering shop in the 1920s

HOBBIES REAP REWARDS

The 1920s and 30s were in contrast to the austere post-war days, and could be described as "Hobbies' Heydays". The investment in plant and retail premises before the First World War was to prove invaluable. During the War the engineering and woodwork departments had been kept working to full capacity - albeit not always manufacturing Hobbies' usual products, and despite the war there had been a very healthy demand for the firm's traditional fretwork products, which had seen, at times, heavy demands on the retail outlets.

Hobbies had invested heavily in their engineering department and this area became the dominant focus of the firm, marking a shift from the woodwork department, which had been the mainstay of Hobbies since its creation. After the War, Hobbies capitalised on the expertise gained in servicing Ministry contracts and were able to gain other contracts to keep their large engineering facility fully occupied. New products were gradually introduced, metal greenhouses have already been mentioned, and there were more exciting developments to come.

During the early 20s, Mr. C. R. Bloxham, Branches Inspector, made several trips to Canada to enlarge the ever increasing export trade which was, by then, being made to that

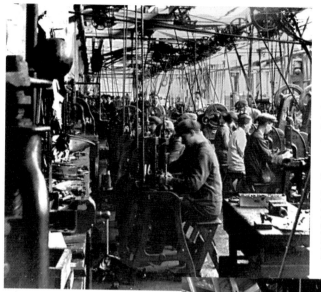

area. When John Henry Skinner first started the company in the 1880s, he imported fret machines from Seneca Falls, in upper New York State, just south of Lake Ontario. Ironically, less than forty years on, business had turned full circle and Hobbies were exporting to the same area!

In 1921, two new directors were appointed to the board. Frank Jewson of The Elms, Mount Pleasant, Norwich, a solicitor; and Bertrand William Jermyn, Northbury, Chase Avenue, King's Lynn, House Furnisher.

CHAIRMAN DIES

On 7th June 1921, Sir Alfred Jermyn died from a heart attack, aged 76. He was the son of a Wymondham farmer and miller and had established a furniture, bedding and household goods store in High Street, King's Lynn, in 1872. In December of 1884 the store suffered a disastrous fire which destroyed property to the value of £25,000. He had been Chairman of Hobbies for 16 years.

Richard Jewson was appointed Chairman of Hobbies Ltd., replacing Sir Alfred Jermyn.

In late April 1922, managers of branches and departments made

Scenes of the 1920s -
Top: The engineering shop
Centre: Drilling machines
Bottom: Capstan lathes

60

their annual tour of the factory to see the new extensions which had been built and to view the up-to-date machinery which had been installed. They were also given a demonstration, on the Neatherd Pond, of two model steam launches which Hobbies were going to put on the market the following year. This, of course, was their introduction to the now famous brand name of Bowman's Models (see chapter 9).

CANADIAN BRANCH OPENS

At a party later that week, held at the King's Head Hotel in Norwich Street, Mr. Richard Jewson asked the assembled managers to wish Mr. Bloxham "bon voyage" on his fifth trip to Canada, hoping for further increases in trade with Canada.

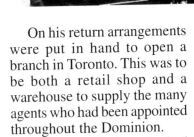

More factory scenes from the 1920s:

Top: Smart headgear worn by this lathe operator!

Centre: Youngsters tempering fretsaw blades

Bottom: The grinding shop

On his return arrangements were put in hand to open a branch in Toronto. This was to be both a retail shop and a warehouse to supply the many agents who had been appointed throughout the Dominion.

Mr. Wm. Clarke, who had joined Hobbies in 1922 and became the first manager of the Brighton branch when it opened in 1923, was chosen to inaugurate and manage the

Toronto branch when it was opened at 45 Colborne. By 1930 the branch had moved to $385\frac{1}{2}$ Yonge Street and the following year to 844 Yonge Street, and by 1935 to 54 Wellington Street West, Toronto. At one time the Toronto branch was publishing its own catalogue of 132 pages.

William Clarke's wife-to-be joined him in Canada in 1928 for their marriage. She once said that William had sent her a postcard from the top of the Empire State Building, which he had visited on the way to take up his new appointment. She thought that to

The general stores, 1925

take the time to think of her and to send her a postcard from such a wonderful place was such a nice gesture that she ought to marry such a considerate man! The Clarkes returned to England in 1930 and Joseph Barberis took over as manager of the Toronto branch.

Left: The Promotion Car
Below: Frank Toyne

MOBILE DEMONSTRATIONS

To increase trade at home Hobbies embarked on an ingenious publicity drive. They had a special Demonstration Car built which was fitted out so that one side would open up allowing plenty of display space for kits and tools, and an area where demonstrations of fretwork could be staged. The vehicle had a crew of two; the driver was Frank Mayfield Toyne, and it travelled all over the country giving demonstrations of fretwork. Whenever possible the vehicle was entered in local carnivals and often took the prize for best decorated vehicle, giving Hobbies valuable free advertising.

Frank Toyne wrote articles in *Hobbies Weekly,* over the signature "FMT", particularly "A Tour Through England", recording the adventures of driving the Demonstration Car around the country. He also wrote about the places of interest in the towns which the Demonstration Car passed through on their Tour of England, ranging from God's House Tower in Southampton to Walbeck Abbey in "The Dukeries", via The Cross at Banbury. His articles also included some of the amusing events which occurred on their travels.

Frank Toyne also used to demonstrate Bowman's steam launches on local yacht ponds to crowds of interested children. When the Demonstration Car made a visit to Southampton, he arranged a race on the yacht pond on Southampton Common for steam launches purchased from Hobbies. The Southampton evening paper recorded: "The enthusiasm and interest shown for nautical sport was emphasised last evening by the large crowd of people - estimated at over 1,000 - who gathered around the yacht pond on Southampton Common to witness a race with "Hobbies" steam launches". The article went on to record that first prize had been awarded to Mr. O. G. Robinson of 41 Argyle Road, Southampton for giving the best all-round performance of the evening with his "Miss America".

Frank Toyne also spoke on an early children's radio broadcast when he extolled the virtues of fretwork, which provided endless things to make, whereas model railways "just required the child to watch the trains go past"!

Packing cases leaving the Supply Department for export in 1925

HOBBIES DIVERSIFY

In early 1924, following their policy of diversification, Hobbies were considering embarking upon one of two engineering projects, manufacturing either metal framed windows or steel tennis rackets. The decision was made to manufacture the tennis rackets. No doubt the enthusiasm of the Managing Director, Richard Jewson, for the sport held some sway in the decision making. He was an accomplished competition standard tennis player, and played competitively into his more mature years. No doubt Crittalls were grateful for that decision as they themselves took up the opportunity for manufacturing metal windows!

John W. Coulter, a prominent tennis player of the mid-20s, promoted Hobbies' "Crescent" steel tennis rackets, saying that on wet courts the balls soon become soaked and heavy which meant speedy death to the best gut and wood rackets. These were affected by atmospheric changes, and the reaction of a racket on a dry day is different to that on a wet day.

Players were reluctant to hit out at a heavy ball with a racket whose gut is soft and loose as they were not prepared to run the risk of having to re-string or even replace their wooden

Right: A 1925 advertisement for Crescent Steel Racket

Below: Making tennis rackets in 1925

WIRE STRUNG

22/6

Postage 9d. extra.

THE CRESCENT STEEL RACKET
DRIVES LIKE THE WIND!

ITS SMALL WIND RESISTANCE GIVES GREATER DRIVING POWER, MORE ACCURATE DIRECTION AND SPIN.

A WIRE-STRUNG RACKET SCIENTIFICALLY PLANNED AND CONSTRUCTED TO GIVE YOU BETTER PLAY.

TRY ONE OUT THIS SEASON.

Send for a free illustrated leaflet to Dept. C.R.

Hobbies Ltd., Dereham, Norfolk
and of Branches, Agents and Sports Dealers Everywhere.

model. The steel strings were half the diameter of the gut ones and the metal surface of the frame was less than that of the wooden counterpart. This resulted in reduced air resistance allowing the delivery of a speedier blow. Some enthusiasts for the steel rackets said that they were so good that gut-and-wood rackets "would not be seen outside a museum ten or twenty years hence". Although the timing projected in this claim was adrift by half a century, it was, nevertheless, fairly accurate. However, at the time, despite constant promotion production only appeared to have lasted for a year or two.

One of the main exponents of the steel racket was Richard Jewson, and in September 1925 it was recorded that it was very wet for the start of the Bungay Tournament. When play was commenced the steel tennis rackets were brought out and Richard Jewson enjoyed some success.

In 1925 Hobbies marketed the largest "kit" they ever made - a three roomed wooden bungalow! This was supplied with all materials cut to size and finished ready for assembly by the purchaser. Reports in the local press, half a century later, revealed that there were still some of the bungalows in existence and still occupied, paying testimony to the quality and value of the original kits.

Above: One of the few surviving examples of a Hobbies' tennis racket

Left: The timber drying sheds

Below: The huge gantry crane at work in 1925

HOBBIES IN COURT

Since the establishment of Home Handicrafts Ltd. by Frank Skinner, brother of Hobbies founder, John Henry Skinner, relations between the two firms had been somewhat acrimonious. Hobbies had enjoyed considerable

time without opposition and probably resented any competition which had the audacity to manifest itself.

On the 31st August 1926 Hobbies were prosecuted by Handicrafts Ltd, of Lister Works, Weedington Road, Kentish Town, London, because, they claimed, a false trade description had been applied to goods offered for sale at 147 Bishopgate, London. The word "Patent"

Left: Selecting timber for the bandsaw
Centre: The bandsaw could handle timber up to 6 feet in diameter
Bottom: The wood turning department in 1925

had been applied to several articles in respect of which a patent had originally been granted, but in every case had then expired. Mr. Alderman W. Phene Neal dismissed the summons as he was satisfied that Hobbies Ltd. had not been guilty of fraudulent intent.

Just two weeks later, in Clerkenwell Magistrates Court, Hobbies retaliated with a summons against Handicrafts Ltd. claiming that a similar false trade description had been applied to goods offered for sale by Handicrafts Ltd. It seems that whilst on holiday in London in July, Mr. Walter Brown, manager of Hobbies' Southampton branch, had visited the retail shop attached to Handicrafts' works in Weedington Road and purchased a

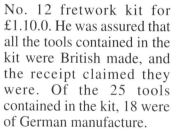

No. 12 fretwork kit for £1.10.0. He was assured that all the tools contained in the kit were British made, and the receipt claimed they were. Of the 25 tools contained in the kit, 18 were of German manufacture.

Later, Mr. Albey Campbell Teamby, an assistant at Hobbies' Bishopgate branch, purchased a No. 5 carpentry tool set and was also assured they were all British made and a receipt made out to that effect. Of the 14 tools, 12 were of German manufacture. Hobbies claimed that German tools were inferior to those manufacture in Britain, and when sold as British would make 150% profit for the seller. Another assistant, from Hobbies' New Oxford Street branch also stated that on August 5th he had purchased a 1A and a 4A fretwork outfit, and was assured that the tools were all of British manufacture and had been assembled on the premises.

Following counter claims by Handicrafts Ltd. that Hobbies had also sold tools and mouldings as being British made but which were in fact of German manufacture, the Magistrate, Mr. Hay Halkett, fined Handicrafts Ltd. £20, with 80 guineas costs.

A similar summons was also taken out by Hobbies Ltd. against Currys Ltd, who had about 130 branches in London, which were supplied by Handicrafts Ltd. The magistrate decided that Currys had been innocent victims in that they had unknowingly purchased German made tool kits believing them to be British made. Nevertheless he

More views of the woodwork department in 1925

felt they should have done more to ascertain the origin of their purchases, therefore he ordered Currys to pay the costs of the case amounting to £21.

Although the fine imposed on Handicrafts Ltd. was considered as relatively minor, Hobbies regarded they had scored a major victory, and to "turn the knife in the wound" had details of the case circulated to all the national newspapers, major provincial newspapers, and trade publications, to maximise on the publicity. On 9th October 1926, newspapers from the Glasgow Herald to the Torbay Herald and Express, and from the Liverpool Post and Mercury to the Yorkshire Observer, all carried practically identical reports of the case.

HANDICRAFTS WIN DAMAGES

In January of 1928 Handicrafts Ltd. successfully sued the Wholesale Traders' Association for the Hardware, Furnishing and Metal Industries Ltd. for libel upon the financial standing and credit worthiness of Handicrafts Ltd. A German firm, Arniz and Hammes, had asked for a credit worthiness reference from the Wholesale Traders' Association, who were in business to supply information about the commercial integrity

Four new fretmachines introduced in the mid 1920s:
left to right, the OK, Imperial and Triumph, and below the Victory

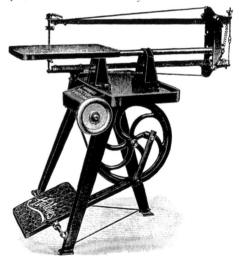

of a firm. The Association advised that the business of Handicraft Ltd. was declining, there was an outstanding County Court judgement for £16.10.0, and did not recommend Handicrafts Ltd as credit worthy for the sum of £200. Handicrafts refuted the allegations, claiming business was increasing year by year; judgement was made against the Wholesale Traders' Association and damages of £450 were awarded to Handicrafts Ltd.

Back in Dereham, in March 1928, Hobbies were again in court, but this time one of their employees was accused of theft. Hector Houghton, a general labourer of Yarmouth, was charged with stealing tools worth £2.2.3 when working as a bench hand at Hobbies between November 1927 and February 1928. Houghton was also charged with stealing a watch and necklace valued at £5.15.0 from Mrs. Bellchamber, the landlady of his lodgings in Dereham, and possessing a revolver without a firearms certificate. Houghton was sentenced to six months hard labour for each of the two theft charges and another month for the firearms offence. The case attracted full coverage in the local press, and no doubt the severity of the sentence served as ample warning to Hobbies' other employees.

FULL EMPLOYMENT AND GOOD WAGES

In September 1927, Hobbies employed 119 staff at Dereham, but by September 1928 numbers had grown to 200, the biggest increase was in the engineering section which expanded from 56 to 111. Office staff in 1928 rose from 10 to 21 and did not vary by more than 2 either way until the outbreak of the Second World War. Staffing levels continued to increase until by the end of 1928 some 227 were employed, but this number dropped to 178 by the following June, and was back up to 227 in December 1929. In the ten years between 1929 and the outbreak of the war numbers fluctuated between 174 and over 200, ending 1939 with 180.

In the mid-20s, Hobbies were paying good wages by local standards. Most men were taking home between £1.15.0 and £2.0.0 per week. Skilled workers earned 1/- per hour for a 47 hour week. Hourly rates varied from $7\frac{1}{2}$d. for younger workers to 1/2 for the top workers in the various departments. Shop foremen and managers were on a special rate and the manager of the engineering department was paid £5.14.0 per week. The top pay packet in

Hobbies' circular saw, 1927

the office was £3.15.0 per week and in the foundry £4.8.8d.

In the autumn of 1928 another new design of fretmachine was launched, called the "Gem". This was constructed entirely of metal, including the top and bottom arms, and was destined to become as popular as its predecessors, the "A1" and the earlier "Briton".

Free-wheel circular saw, 1927

The Gem fretmachine, introduced in 1928

Although, when first launched, it was fitted with the usual ornate foundry-cast treadle platform, incorporating the Hobbies logo in a pierced design, it was later replaced by a more utilitarian pressed steel fabrication. Such was the cost of progress!

Articles in *Hobbies Weekly* were continuing to expand their wide range of interest, but by far the two most popular subjects were cycling and radio, or rather "wireless" as it was called at the time. Plans for making the "Hobbies Three" wireless were published in *Hobbies Weekly* and in the 1929 annual catalogue, which consisted of 280 pages and cost 9d. For 4d. a full size plan could be obtained, together with instructions and details of the necessary components which could be obtained locally or by mail order from Hobbies. Also available were kits for making wireless cabinets and speakers. Very popular at this time were kits for making

In the 1930s Hobbies sold many of their products to tobacco companies who offered them to smokers in exchange for coupons

gramophones, either a table model costing £1.10.0, or a cabinet model with storage space for records at £2.16.0, which could be ordered from Hobbies.

The Hobbies 1931 annual catalogue extended to a record 288 pages and cost 9d. Among the many and varied tools and materials on offer were electric drives to fit most of their available range of fret machines and the "I.D.L.", another new fret machine.

A new toy, "The Half-Mile Flyer", was offered for the first time for the budding aeronautical enthusiast. Geoffrey Bowman Jenkins (see chapter 9) had perfected the means of driving model boats by long rubber bands, and the aeroplane appears to have been a development of this method of propulsion.

The Half-Mile Flyer

JOHN GREEN DIES

On Thursday 19th February 1931 John Green died at the age of 83 years at his home at Kew, where he had resided for 18 years. He had lived in Dereham from 1884 to 1913 when he went into semi-retirement and moved to Kew so that he could enjoy the amenities of the gardens nearby which were so close to his heart.

He was chairman of the National Sweet Pea Society, honorary treasurer of the National Chrysanthemum and National Dahlia Societies, and a member of the Council of the National Rose Society. He had served for over 20 years on the Floral Committee of the Royal Horticultural Society, and was co-founder of the London Dahlia Union and became its first president.

At Dereham, he had served on the old Local Board and on the Urban District Council, which replaced the Local Board, and became its chairman. He was a member of the Sondes Lodge of Freemasons, and retained a keen interest in that body up till his death.

GOVERNMENT CONTRACTS

During the late 20s and 30s, Hobbies held a number of contracts for producing bomb gear for the Government and many foreign countries. The largest bomb carrier they produced was for Halifax aircraft for carrying 8,000 lb. bombs. Hobbies also produced

thousands of $8\frac{1}{2}$ lb. practice bombs on mass production lines, dummy bombs, dummy men for testing parachutes, transit plugs for smoke bombs, and many wooden boxes for detonators, instruments, magnetos and tools, etc. Bomb carriers of different designs were produced along with control gear, fuse wires, armour-piercing bomb vanes, drogue release gear, and engine spares, etc. As a consequence of these contracts, and the buoyant sales of fretwork kits and ancillary items (over 10 million fretsaw blades were manufacture in 1931 alone), the factory enjoyed full employment and prosperous times.

HOBBIES LEAGUE FORMED

In 1931 "The Hobbies League" was formed. The declared objects of the League was to bring together and help as much as possible anybody and everybody interested in fretwork and woodwork. Members of the League were encouraged to correspond with other fretworkers and make friends with one another either in their own district or on the other side of the world. Local clubs were also formed where members of the League could meet regularly where they were encouraged to pool materials and work together to produce models or articles for sale to raise funds for the club.

Prospective members were required to apply for a booklet which explained all membership details and supplied a pattern for a test panel which had to be cut out and submitted to Hobbies to prove that every member was capable of handling a fretsaw satisfactorily. Cost of membership was 6d, or for those living overseas 1/-, and members received a "striking 2-colour certificate" and a lapel badge. Additionally,

members could purchase a set of three pencils which were printed with the name of the member in gold for 8d. and a rubber stamp for marking notepaper with the League's badge. Fretworkers who made items to sell could purchase a 10 x 8 ins. showcard for 2d., which could be hung in the window and proclaimed "Fretwork Cut Here". Design No. 1898 was available at 4d to enable the League member to make a special frame for his or her certificate, and for 2d. extra a colour transfer of the Leagues' badge could be purchased for fixing at the top of the frame.

Hobbies maintained a register of those willing to undertake fretwork for profit and names were passed on to those making enquiries. Members were sent periodic bulletins, and news of the activities of the League were frequently published in *Hobbies Weekly*. Special competitions were also arranged which were restricted to League members.

In October 1931 *Hobbies Weekly* published their most ambitious project to date - details of how to make a full-size glider! The writer, F. J. Camm, claimed the glider was safe and capable of making short glides at a height of 40ft or 50 ft, "even more if you have access to a fairly steep hill"! The author further suggested that the reader "should not go to the trouble of erecting a catapulting device yet"! The glider had a wing span of 25ft and a fuselage length of just over 14ft, and required the craftsman to have access to only a plane,

saw, hammer and chisel, with no parts requiring the use of a lathe. No doubt many fretworkers saw this as a welcome diversion from the usual run-of-the-mill pipe racks, photograph frames and wool winders. Unfortunately it is not on record how many gliders were made or how many intrepid aeronautical fretworkers took to the skies above their workshops!

Hobbies' 1932 annual catalogue achieved an even higher record level of page content when it was extended to 304 pages, still at the cost of 9d. Wireless and gramophones still dominated the project section, as well as musical instruments including a guitar, ukulele, Fiji fiddle, ukulele banjo and a Jap fiddle, for which designs were available for between 4d. and 9d. depending on the instrument. Full details were given for making a "Tube-O-Phone", an instrument similar to a xylophone but using tubes of various length instead of flat "keys". This was supported on an oak table with elegant twisted legs, for which a kit of planed wood, including ready turned legs, could be purchased from Hobbies for 11/6. This did not include the table top, which cost an additional 4/-. The set of 25 tubes, cut, tuned and polished, cost 13/6, and various other accessories such as a pair of beaters at 6d. and a set of hinges at 2d., were also available.

DEATH OF HERBERT JEWSON

On 30th November 1932 another of Hobbies' long serving stalwarts, Herbert Jewson, died at the age of 68 at his home at Earith, Huntingdonshire. He was buried in the family vault in Bluntisham Meeting House.

Herbert Jewson was a clever and skilled engineer who had controlled the engineering department until 1930. He had worked in Egypt and Persia, and, in 1887, shortly after the formation of Hobbies, was appointed the company's chief engineer. He invented many unique and useful pieces of machinery and tools for the specialist production of Hobbies' range of fretwork machines, tools and equipment. Among these was an ingenious machine for the manufacture of fretsaw blades which, before the end of the 1890s, enabled Hobbies to cease importing German made blades and become the only producer of fretsaw blades in Great Britain.

Herbert Jewson had been a councillor and chairman of Dereham Urban District Council. In 1922 he received Prince Henry, brother of King George VI, when he performed the unveiling of Dereham War Memorial. He was president of the Dereham branch of the YMCA and devoted his energies to the men's side of the Adult School before the First World War. He was an expert skater and enjoyed golf, bowls, rambling and tennis.

He was an active Freemason being a member of Sondes Lodge No. 996 and the Harry Sparkes Chapter. Herbert Jewson was Worshipful Master of Sondes Lodge in 1905 and received Provincial Honours as PGSB in 1907. He was an elder of the Chapter and attained the rank of PZ.

MORE NEW PRODUCTS

By 1934 the title of the annual catalogue had changed to the grander sounding "Handbook", the page content had decreased to 268 pages and the price had reduced to 6d., two-thirds of the previous cost. The 1934 issue heralded the distinctive "Anchor" fret machine, which claimed an innovation in cutting and running capabilities. This was made possible by utilising a flexible steel band, running over ball bearing pulleys, to operate the saw blade in a true vertical stroke. A motorised bench model was available as well as a traditional treadle version. The latter was supported on an anchor shaped base plate and the foot treadle carried an embossed anchor with the Hobbies logo superimposed over the top. The machines gained their name from the shape of the oscillating cam which supplied movement to the steel band, and cost £3.15.0 for the bench model and £4.15.0 for the treadle version. In comparison the two popular machines, "Gem" and "A1" sold for £2.0.0 and £2.15.0 respectively.

The Anchor Fretmachine

Other introductions included a range of "Norfolk" model yachts in four sizes from 12 ins to 24 ins long, priced from 6/6 to 25/-, and the "Clipper" range from 24 ins to 36 ins. at 47/6 to 90/-. These were supplied as ready-to-sail models, the "Clipper" range being made from Gaboon mahogany with a traditional built-up hull. Sailing model boats had become a very popular pastime - many seaside resorts and inland parks created a model yacht pond where boys (and their sons) could enjoy the sport.

Table tennis, previously known as "Ping-Pong" had also become very popular, and clubs and leagues were formed to cater for the many enthusiasts. Hobbies made and supplied two sizes of table, 8ft x 4ft at 30/- or match size 9ft x 5 ft at 40/-, plus a table tennis outfit comprising net, six balls and two cork faced bats for 5/-.

JOHN SKINNER RETIRES - BUT STARTS AGAIN

In the 1932, John Henry Skinner retired from business life in Durban and returned to England, only to create another firm, Skinner, Thomas & Co. This firm was based at Imperial House, South Street, London, EC2, and was formed into a limited liability company in 1935; in addition to John Skinner, the directors included his son, Mr. R. S. Skinner, and Mr. R. M. Thomas, who was also assistant managing director.

The firm manufactured plywood and veneers, and, whilst output was increased annually, could not cope with demand. The

John and Bessie Skinner in retirement

company purchased land in Durban, South Africa, and erected a large factory, which was completed by the end of April 1937. John Skinner's son went out to South Africa to manage the firm, and later in 1937 all the equipment needed for the new timber mill was sent out to Durban. Mr. R. M. Thomas also went to join the firm, leaving J. H. Skinner in sole charge of the London office, where he supervised the buying of the necessary raw materials to keep the factory supplied. The Durban enterprise more than doubled the firm's capacity and specialised in manufacturing high quality plywood and veneered panels, flush doors and parquet flooring in teak and mahogany.

In 1938 another of John Henry Skinner's original employees died. Arthur Winter had joined J. H. Skinner & Co. in 1884 at the age of 12. He was employed in the sawmills and later was in charge of that department. He was well known in the district, and over a wider area, as a skilled timber buyer. He was taken ill at work and died later on March 5th 1938.

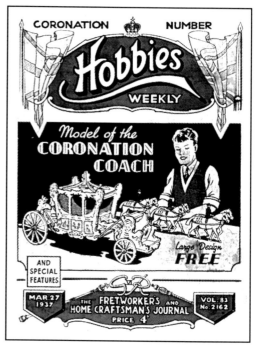

In 1937 the Coronation of King George VI provided Hobbies with many opportunities to publish appropriate plans, including this fine model of the Coronation coach

During the late 20s and the 30s the board of directors changed very little. In 1928 Edward Charles Annison Green was appointed managing director, and in 1931 Frank Jewson became vice-chairman. Edward Stratton Aslett, of Yew Lodge, Bessels Green, Sevenoaks, Kent, an engineer, joined the board in 1937 but resigned in 1939 and was replaced by Arthur Reginald Pratt, of Palmer House, Litcham, King's Lynn, who was the company secretary.

The last Handbook of the decade still cost only 6d. for 284 pages and introduced the new "Marvel" fretmachine. This had a welded steel frame and a piston arrangement to provide a true vertical stroke, and was available in both an electric driven bench model and a treadle version. This was the first machine to be fitted with a pressed steel treadle platform as standard from the launch date. A similar pressed steel platform had been fitted to the "Gem" some years after it first appeared on the market in 1928. The "Marvel" cost 22/6 for the bench model (motor 84/- extra), or 27/6 for the treadle model. The "Gem" had been reduced in price to 35/-, and the "A1" to 52/6.

By the end of the 30s rumblings of the threat of another war grew louder. On 1st September 1939 Hitler invaded Poland. But, as will be seen, Hobbies took this Second World War in its stride, as it did the Great War of 1914-18. Two days later Neville Chamberlain announced, in a broadcast to the nation, that Britain had declared war on Germany.

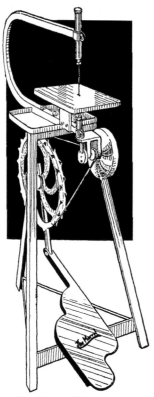

The Marvel Fretmachine

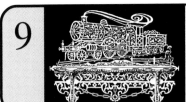

9

Full Steam Ahead

FOLLOWING the Great War, because of the intense anti-German feeling, the toy industry adopted an effective slogan, "British Toys for British Boys", and the industry responded well to the challenge of satisfying the market which had previously been largely dependant on cheap German imports from firms such as Gebr. Bing and Marklin. Fortunately the British toy makers did not copy the cheap imports but instead invested in the manufacture of well designed and well made products. It has already been reported in Chapter 8 of what happened to a supplier who was passing off cheap German imports as being British made.

During the war, Geoffrey Bowman Jenkins, an ingenious and inventive toy maker, had been making and selling toys from a small shop in Northcote Road, not far from Clapham Common, London, under the name of Woodcraft Patents Co. His preference was for mechanical toys, especially steam driven toys, although his first patent, No. 123464 granted in 1919, covered the means of driving a locomotive by elastic.

By this time the activities of Geoffrey Bowman Jenkins had come to the notice of the Board of Directors of Hobbies Ltd. Since the turn of the century Hobbies had imported German-made toy steam engines and, in

Geoffrey Bowman Jenkins

response to the anti-German hysteria which had enveloped the country, needed to find an alternative source of supply, preferably British. Mr. Jenkins fitted the bill admirably and was invited to come to Dereham to discuss the possibility of a joint venture.

PROTOTYPES SAIL THE NEATHERD POND

In 1922 he supplied prototypes of two models to Hobbies. These were demonstrated, on the Neatherd pond at the end of April, to the managers of Hobbies' branches as examples of new products which Hobbies were going to market the following year.

Geoffrey Bowman Jenkins was impressed with the offer made by Hobbies. Part of the engineering department was to be leased to him, and Hobbies would market his products through their firmly established sales network of *Hobbies Weekly* (then selling 70,000 copies per week), their annual handbook with a similar circulation and their chain of retail shops and agents. So Geoffrey Bowman Jenkins made the move to Dereham early in 1923; some older Hobbies employees tell the tale of how he arrived in Dereham from London on a motorcycle with Len Stokes who worked for him in London!

The first employees of Bowman Models

Altogether three key workers moved from London with Geoffrey Bowman Jenkins and began production of a small range of sailing yachts and compressed air driven boats together with the two steam driven boats, under the trade name of "Bowman Models". The manufacturing operation really was one of assembly only as wooden hulls were made in Hobbies' woodworking department, cylinders, gear wheels, flywheels and other small parts were purchased from Bullpits of Birmingham and other manufacturers, and tin-plate parts such as cabs and chassis were fabricated in Hobbies' engineering works.

Of the three men who moved up to Dereham with Jenkins, one returned to London.

A second, Albert Percy Fulcher, claimed compensation for an injury. He had cut the index finger of his right hand on a circular saw on May 30th 1923 and could not follow his trade as a toolmaker, So in September he sued Geoffrey Bowman Jenkins for compensation for financial loss as, instead of earning £3.7.6 per week as a skilled tool maker, he could only earn between 37/- and 40/- per week as a labourer. He claimed he also lost income of 5/- per week as a pianist. Geoffrey Bowman Jenkins was not insured so was required by law to compensate the injured man for loss of earnings. The court awarded the plaintiff, then living at 41 Exeter Street, Norwich, compensation of £1 per week.

The third man, Len Stokes, stayed to take charge of a small workforce of about a dozen youngsters recruited locally.

STEAM BOATS ARE GREAT SUCCESS

Also in 1923 Geoffrey Bowman Jenkins was granted his second patent, No. 208319, which related to "Improvements in toy steam boats and the like". The range of steam driven boats was increased to four, *"Swallow"* (20 ins. long), *"Snipe"* (23 ins. long) and *"Seahawk"* and *"Eagle"* (both 28 ins. long). Early prototypes were tested on the Neatherd Pond and frequently someone had to wade in to retrieve a broken-down model. It was not unknown for models to explode whilst undergoing tests, which led to the installation of proficient safety valves! Gradually the boats

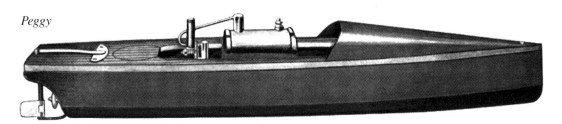

Peggy

manufactured by Geoffrey Bowman Jenkins gained a reputation among enthusiasts for being solidly and well made with a power for size ratio better than anything similar on the market. As well as Hobbies' own publications, advertisements were also placed in publications such as *Boys Own Paper* and *Meccano Magazine.* The demand encouraged the introduction of four more steam driven boats with the nostalgic names of *"Miss America", "Pioneer"* and *"Peggy"* (named after Jenkins' eldest daughter) which was the most expensive in the range at 22/6, also a tiny *"Peter Pan".* Two of the engines could be purchased separately, either for installation in boats made by customers or for driving other models.

Pioneer with super-heated engine

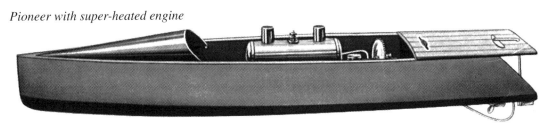

Encouraged by the strong demand for the steam driven boats, marketed under either the Bowman Models or Hobbies labels, and sometimes jointly under the Hobbies-Bowman brand label, a new factory unit was built in 1926 by Hobbies and leased to Geoffrey Bowman Jenkins. The range of models was also expanded to include railway engines and rolling stock finished in the various colours of the main line railway companies. The engines were hand finished in heat resisting varnishes and polished brass, and, although they were not built to scale, they ran on "0" gauge track, and were very powerful for their size. In 1928 a steam driven tug was added to the range of boats but was not named.

At the British Industries Fair at White City, London, in 1929 the Bowman Models were a great success. One Bowman 4-4-0 engine covered 183 actual miles hauling six coaches. It was refilled every forty minutes and covered a journey of one and a half miles on each filling. It cost 35/-! Also at the British Industries Fair, Geoffrey Bowman Jenkins exhibited his newly patented (No. 331666) rust-proofed steel railway track which was mounted on wooden sleepers.

The stationery steam engines were at first mounted on wooden bases but later metal bases were used. At this time Meccano had probably reached its peak in popularity and supplied small clockwork and electric motors with their larger kits. The inventive Geoffrey

Miss America

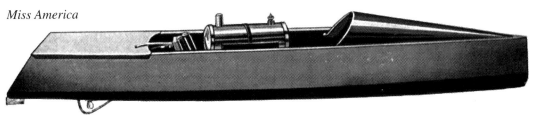

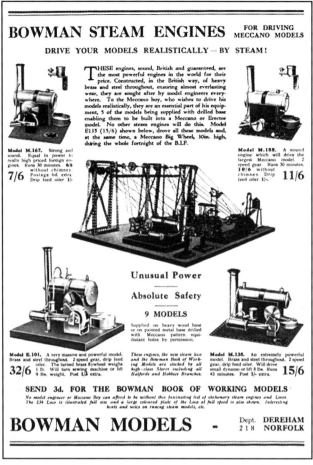

The range of Bowman's steam engines advertised in Boy's Own Paper in 1928

Jenkins saw an ideal opportunity which he was quick to grasp. He simply drilled the metal bases of his steam engines with 5/32 in. diameter holes at 1/2 inch centres so that Bowman steam engines could be incorporated into Meccano models, some of which were extremely ambitious and sizeable creations. The engines were priced between 5/9 and £1.17.6, and the range included a patented dynamo, which produced a bright light utilising a 2-volt bulb, at 7/6.

The "Demon" engine, made by Bowman's but sold under the Hobbies trade mark

The full range of Bowman models by now also included spring driven racing launches which were wound by means of a "gramophone" type winding handle. The *"Ajax"* and *"Comet"* models sold for 22/6 and 20/- respectively. The new spring drive was a considerable improvement on ordinary clockwork motors and combined long runs with incredible speed. If a traditional clockwork version was preferred Bowmans produced the *"Tiger"* at 17/6.

The Pioneer marine steam engine, made to fit into enthusiast's own models

DEPRESSION BRINGS DIVERSIFICATION

The depression years of the early thirties were to have a devastating effect on the Bowman business. Although Bowman's products were of very good quality, people had little money available for toys. The firm first tackled the problem of dropping sales by

Above: Cover of Bowman's Catalogue - essential bedtime reading for most boys!

Right: Just two of the exciting pages inside the catalogue

introducing a range of "Aeroboats". These would run for up to four times longer than traditional clockwork racing boats and could be fully wound in 15 seconds. The *"Aeroboat II"* would run for 9 minutes and cost 15/6, whilst the *"Aeroboat I"* ran for between 12 and 15 minutes and cost 17/6. Other fast racing boats included the *"Whippet"*, 29 ins. long, at 9/6, the *"Greyhound"*, 30 ins. long for 8/6, and the *"Whirlwind"*, manufactured from light wood, rubber driven, 27 ins. long, at an amazing cost of only 1/3!

However, the continued economic situation, coupled with a failure to produce in the right season, resulted in falling sales and the firm diversified into chemistry sets, induction "shocking" coils and model aeroplanes. Geoffrey Bowman Jenkins also applied his inventive mind to other areas of mechanics and came up with a

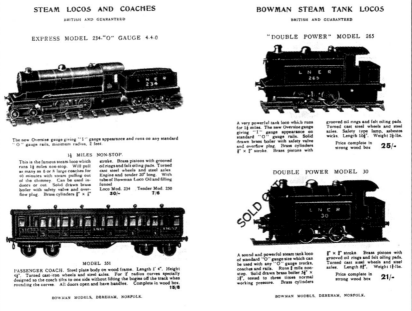

means for producing electricity free! This involved a small hydraulic motor which was fastened to a water tap by a patent grip. The pressure of the water would turn the motor at 5,000 r.p.m. and would generate sufficient power to work a small dynamo which would, in turn, generate enough electricity to light at least six 1.5 volt bulbs "which could be led to any part of the house". The power was also sufficient to drive a sewing machine or work fairly large models. Obviously Geoffrey Bowman Jenkins did not suffer the water restrictions of the present time!

An adaptation of this invention was the mechanical tooth brush which Geoffrey Bowman Jenkins patented (Nos. 369253 and 369600). Neither inventions was destined to become the saviour of the firm largely because the steel jaws which were part of the tap fixing system caused severe damage to water taps!

The most wonderful model steam loco ever made!

SPECIFICATION:

Bowman Express Loco Model 234. Solid brass and steel throughout and fully illustrated. BOILER. — Heavy seamless brass tested to 5 times working pressure. New Bowman safety valve. Overflow and fire filling to correct level. CYLINDERS. — Drawn brass *F & F*. Solid brass pistons with grooved oil-rings. Special felt oiling pads. FRAME. — Heavy steel plate. WHEELS. — Turned steel. LAMP. — Safety type. asbestos wicks. Goes out if overturned. GAUGE "O." — For 2' radius. PACKING. — Complete in strong box with tube of oil. filling funnel and full instructions.

NOTE THE MASSIVE PROPORTIONS:

Length of Engine and Tender, 1 ft. 8 ins.

PRICE OF LOCO:

27/6

TENDER: 7/6 extra

Post U.K. 1/-, abroad 4/-

183 MILES! This is the wonder Bowman Loco which pulled 6 large coaches (as illustrated) for a distance of 183 miles during the B.I.F. It was re-fuelled every 40 minutes, a journey of 1½ miles. A £5 foreign steam engine refused to pull half the load and ran for 12 minutes only, on one filling.

A NEW CRAZE. Think of the joy such an engine can add to your railway system! It runs on your own "O" gauge track and pulls your rolling stock 1½ miles amidst clouds of steam from the chimney and the true exhaust steam sound of a real locomotive. Owing to its unusual power, an outdoor steam railway is now possible. Here real journeys can be accomplished, and you can build cuttings, embankments, tunnels and bridges in a most realistic manner.

2/- DEPOSIT SECURES YOUR LOCO FOR XMAS. The demand for this loco is so great that we may be sold out by Xmas. Make sure of yours now—your dealer will reserve it for you for 2/- deposit. If he does not stock Bowman Models, send his name and P.O. 2/-, when we will reserve it for you.

Send 3d. for the Bowman **WONDER BOOK OF WORKING MODELS** A fascinating list of steam engines from 6/6 and full details of this loco, illustrated full size and in colours. Notes on running, etc.

Ask your dealer to show you this Bowman Loco MODEL 234. This loco, Bowman steam engines and wonder book are obtainable from all Halfords and Hobbies branches.

ABSOLUTELY SAFE

←——1 foot 8 inches——→
SAME SIZE AS USUAL £6·0·0 MODELS

READ THESE UNSOLICITED TESTIMONIALS.
Guaranteed Genuine.

"I have a £4 10 0 steam loco made by . . . . and also one of your models. I have never been so delighted with an engine as yours. The other is an 'also ran.' . . . There is not an engine at the price to touch yours.—all my chums say so." (M. H., Bristol.)

"I have run your loco three times and on the third trial, although I did not completely fill lamp, it drew 16 wagons for half an hour. I must say I did not expect a new engine putting up so surprising a performance as this." (S. H., Annfield Plain)

BOWMAN MODELS · · Dept. DEREHAM 217 NORFOLK

JENKINS LEAVES HOBBIES

Jenkins severed his association with Bowmans and Hobbies in 1935. He purchased a small meadow at South Green, Dereham, built a small factory, and went into partnership with his cousin, Capt. Bernard A. Smart, who had been involved for the previous five years with Mr. Warboys in selling Bowman engines. Production of gramophones, under the company name of "Jenkins Productions Limited", was successful, and sold well to cigarette manufacturers such as "Ardath" and "Kensistas" for exchange for coupons. The manufacture of the gramophone cases eventually led Jenkins Productions into manufacturing reproduction antique furniture, and the company name was changed to "Jentique", a combination of "Jenkins" and "antique" - but that is another story!

In the meantime Hobbies were left without a manufacturer of steam engines, a product which they thought still had great potential. Later in 1935 the directors of Hobbies made contact with another Geoffrey - Geoffrey Malin - at the British Industries Fair in Castle Bromwich. Malin had become an engineer with the Austin car firm after leaving school. Later during the war he served in the Navy but after being torpedoed twice was invalided out of the service with shell shock. He then joined the Dunlop Rubber Company as Chief Engineer of their own power station and gained a reputation for excessive efficiency; he

Obviously the problem of falling sales was of concern to Hobbies and it would appear that their relationship with Geoffrey Bowman Jenkins at this time was less than harmonious.

By the mid-thirties he had turned his attention to gramophones. He adapted his spiral spring invention, previously used to power model boats, to drive gramophone motors. Because the spring had to be enclosed in a tube 20 ins. long the motors had to be contained in a cabinet and were not suitable for portable or table models.

Left: The headline of this 1928 advertisement sums up the feelings of most Bowman enthusiasts!

Below: The "Hipower" motor powered from the tap!

was known among his staff as "Mad Malins". After a while Malin decided to set up on his own and established a garage business in 1924. However, the depression years forced him back into employment as a vehicle inspector for a few months but he yearned to become self-employed once again. So he created a workshop at the bottom of his garden, installed a few basic machine tools which he powered by an old Citroen car engine, and called the firm "G. M. Patents Co.", even though he had never held a patent in his life! He came up with the idea of a ball-race turntable which could be incorporated into Meccano models and other construction kits. He also manufactured a range of high quality, solid brass propellers for model boats which were sold exclusively by Hobbies. This initial connection proved particularly useful in the development of Malin's company.

MAMOD IS BORN

When Malin met the directors of Hobbies at the 1935 British Industries Fair he was asked to make a range of engines to fill the gap left by the withdrawal of Geoffrey Bowman Jenkins. Malin grasped the challenge, confident that being only toys they would not present any problems to an engineer experienced with the real thing! With his limited facilities he was unable initially to undertake such a comprehensive range once produced by Bowman Models, but in early 1936 produced a range of four stationery steam engines. All were badged with the Hobbies logo, and were the *"SE1"*, *"SE2"* and *"SE3"* single cylinder engines plus the twin-cylinder *"SE4"*. A marine engine, the *"ME1"*, followed shortly

afterwards. The design of the engines followed fairly closely the style of the Bowman models and 576 were manufactured somewhat laboriously in the first year in a small, cramped workshop, with only one or two part-time workers to assist. Geoffrey Malins was quick to realise that Hobbies need not be his only outlet, and what was needed was a more suitable name for his firm than G. M. Patents Co. It was Geoffrey Malin's wife, Clarrie, who devised the new name. She combined "Ma" from Malins with "Mod" from models to create the name that is now synonymous with model steam engines the world over - Mamod.

Still in production after a chequered history of take-overs Mamod produces only a fraction of the output that was achieved in the firm's heyday. Unfortunately, in these days of the computer and micro chips, youngsters have no interest in steam, and the models have progressed from being toys to nostalgic collectors pieces for enthusiastic adults.

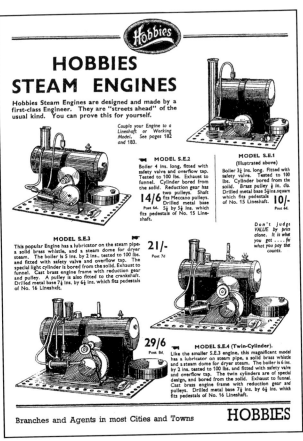

The first four steam engines made by Mamod and sold under the Hobbies trade mark

10 War, Peace, and a Celebration

FOLLOWING the outbreak of war, the staff at Hobbies was decimated. Those who were members of the Territorial Army were the first to be called up for service, quickly followed by those who fitted the criteria of the time. Many of Hobbies' tradesmen were in reserved occupations, which meant they were not called up to serve in the forces, but were sent instead to work at other factories throughout the country on priority munitions work. But the Dereham factory was soon working round the clock to cope with Ministry contracts.

The danger of enemy air attack was a very real threat. Geographically, Dereham is almost in the centre of Norfolk. The town was surrounded by airfields, which were responsible either for launching bomb raids on German targets or fighter attacks on enemy aircraft. The railway was also at the centre of three radial lines serving the surrounding country, and the factories and offices stood astride the main line. Two particularly punishing air raids took place on Norwich on the nights of 27th/28th and 29th/30th April 1942. These were part of the infamous Baedeker Blitz, launched by Hitler as retaliation for RAF bombing raids on the ancient German city of Lübeck. Hitler was intent on destroying important historical cities, and over 297 high-explosive bombs, weighing more than 95 tons, and thousands of incendiaries were dropped on Norwich during the two nights of bombing. The sky glowed red under a huge pall of black smoke as Norwich burned. A total of 231 people were killed and 689 were wounded, incalculable damage was done to shops, businesses and homes. On the second night all available fire appliances from the county were called in to assist in controlling the inferno. The Dereham Fire Brigade attended, also the Hobbies Fire Brigade trailer pump.

During the war there were well over 1,000 alerts on the town's siren - sometimes three and four a day. At first work had to be stopped frequently and this disrupted production. Later a system of localised warning was devised which reduced the disruption. A small

A wartime Hobbies exhibition stand - "somewhere in England"

corrugated iron shelter was constructed on the roof of the factory, which was manned, when the general alert was sounded, by two employees trained to spot enemy aircraft. If one was heard or seen approaching the town they warned the workers below to take cover, and the 24 hour day and night shifts continued with minimum disturbance.

HOBBIES ESCAPES DAMAGE

In spite of the almost daily sound of bombs dropping nearby, the town was fortunate in suffering little damage. On one occasion a stick of incendiaries were strung out down through the station, but none fell on the many acres of ground covered by Hobbies' factory and offices, and miraculously no single injury was sustained by any of the employees due to enemy action.

Kenneth Scott Jewson, Engineer, of Libra, Beetley Common, Dereham, and William Lawrence Fisher, Engineer, of Lorina, King's Road, Dereham, were appointed to the board of directors on 2nd September 1942. Major A. R. Pratt was away on active service with the army in North Africa, and later in Italy. During November 1944 another new director, James Laffan Hanly, a boot and shoe manufacturer, of Inverleith, Lime Tree Road, Norwich, was appointed to the board.

Kenneth Scott Jewson

The 1940 Hobbies Handbook, which was printed and distributed at the end of 1939, ran to the usual 284 pages at a cost of 6d., and over 100,000 copies were issued. The usual free plan was included with the Handbook, and was for building a 36 in. long model of Buckingham Palace. For the first six months of the year, readers were able to send in a coupon to claim a free plan to enable them to build a 24 in. electrically-driven model of H.M.S. Hood. Inside, continuing the war theme, instructions were given for making a working model A.A. gun.

William Lawrence Fisher

Due to the paper shortage, the 1942 Handbook had to be reduced drastically to 104 pages, but still cost 6d. The advertising pages were reduced in number, but pages devoted to war models were considerably extended. The free design, given with the Handbook, was for making a model of a Mark IVa Medium Cruiser Tank. Elsewhere in the Handbook could be found either detailed instructions or plans for making eight scale model war planes, a six-wheel army lorry, six warships, a working model searchlight unit, a working model 4.2 heavy gun,

James Laffan Hanly

MODEL 4.2 HEAVY GUN

DESIGN No. 2317

Not a midget model—but 20 ins. long with 12-in. barrel. With ingenious but simple mechanism for firing small "shells".

Design—Price **4d.**; postage **1d.**

Materials—Panels of Wood, with turned wood gun, beading, round rod, wire, screw eyes, and hook for handle **8/2**; post free **8/9**.

We regret we cannot supply the turned wood gun apart from the complete parcel.

WORKING MODEL ANTI-AIRCRAFT GUN

DESIGN No. 2296

This fine working model actually fires "shells" made from $\frac{3}{16}$ in. dowel rod. The gun can be elevated to almost any angle, and can be swung round for direction.

Design—Price **4d.**; postage **1d.**

Materials—For making this model, we supply Panels of suitable Wood, with dowel rod, turned wood gun ready for fitting, bolt, washers, and screws, **8/6**; postage **7d.**

We cannot supply the turned wood gun apart from the complete parcel.

MOUNTED ANTI-AIRCRAFT GUN

This model has the same firing mechanism as the gun shown above. The gun is swivelled on a carrier, and can be turned in any direction, and elevated through a wide angle. Size of completed model, 18 ins. long.

DESIGN No. 2283

Design—Price **4d.**; postage **1d.**

Materials—We supply Panels of Wood, with dowel rod, turned gun, flat and round-head screws, bolt with wing nut and washers, screw eyes, hinges, chain, wire, and material for mudguards. The set **10/3**, post free **10/10**.

The turned wood gun is not obtainable apart from the complete parcel. Rubber tyres cannot now be supplied.

Armament projects for the budding soldier from Hobbies' 1944 handbook

two anti-aircraft guns, and an R.A.F. refuelling tender. The only projects included in the Handbook which were not connected with the war were a model galleon and a wool winder!

TORONTO BRANCH CLOSES

Because of the difficulties in getting supplies across the Atlantic, due to attacks by German U-boats, the Toronto branch had to be closed down in 1942. A very sad blow had been dealt to Canadian fretwork enthusiasts by a distant enemy.

By 1944 the Handbook had been reduced to 68 pages, but the price remained at 6d. Throughout the war years the cover picture remained the same, obviously to save cost and labour. The same basic war-dominated theme continued, a scale model Liberator bomber being the free design with the 1944 Handbook. The range of treadle fretsaws had been reduced to only two, the ever popular A1 and the Triumph. *Hobbies Weekly* was being produced to the extent of the paper ration, but nevertheless was being despatched to no less than 48 countries, and achieved a circulation of 50,000 copies, including home consumption.

Whilst the free design accompanying the 1945 Handbook was for a working model excavator, the projects continued to be dominated by war subjects, such as

1945 views of:
Top: The sawmills
Centre: The huge bandsaw
Bottom: The woodwork department

85

Top: Woodwork department
Centre: Walter Basham takes
bags of saw-dust and shavings
to the tip in Swanton Road
Bottom: View of the foundry

model planes, which included just about everything flying at that time, like the Lancaster, Mosquito, Thunderbolt, Typhoon, Bristol Beaufighter, Halifax Bomber, Hawker Hurricane, Defiant, Spitfire,

Lysander, Lockheed Lightning, Mitchell Bomber, Sunderland Flying Boat, Westland Whirlwind, Boston, Ventura, Albacore, Boeing Flying Fortress, Wellington and Liberator. The enthusiast of sea going armament was catered for by designs for the King George V Battleship, Southampton Cruiser, Tribal Class Destroyer, Corvette, Torpedo Boat, Shark Submarine, and Aircraft Carrier. Land based equipment was restricted to a model Jeep, Mark IVa Cruiser Tank, Bren Carrier, 6-wheeled Army Lorry, Searchlight Unit and working models of a Gun, a 4.2 Heavy Gun, and an Anti-Aircraft Gun!

In July 1945 Sidney Remington Rudd, who had joined the firm in 1900,

took over as Company Secretary. He had previously served as the firm's accountant in charge of Head Office, then as Assistant Secretary from 1942, and was responsible for dealing with the problems of increased pressure of work brought about by large and demanding Government contracts, and the severe limitations of staffing.

PEACE ARRIVES

When peace came, a smooth return to normal production was made, although shortages of some materials restricted output for a while. The most satisfying alteration, no doubt, was the removal of black-out paint from the glass roofs, allowing staff to work in daylight for the first time for several years. The most welcome event was the return of workers who had served in the forces, particularly those who had been incarcerated in German and Japanese prisoner-of-war camps. Regrettably some did not return. Some of those who had been working in reserved occupations had their return delayed by being called-up into the services for a two year period of duty.

Among those who returned was Leslie Potter. In 1946 he came back to work on the assembly line for 87/- per week, and was shortly to commence his trade union and local

Above: Toolroom, Reg Cox (2nd from left), Jack Laskey (4th from left), Geoffrey Sadd (extreme right)

Right: Harry Tooke (left), Jack Laskey (right) in the toolroom

Below: Operating capstan lathes in 1945, Phylis Warnes (left foreground), Beryl Moy (behind her), Sidney Harbour (right foreground)

government career. He was elected AEU shop steward, a post he occupied for the following 21 years, 13 of which he also served as convenor. He was also to take on the office of District Secretary, and later succeeded Herbert Andrews as Branch Secretary.

After the war, Major A. Pratt (Managing Director) and, among others, Lawrence Fisher and John

Green (both directors), set about restoring the firm to normal peace-time trading. Good quality toys had disappeared from the shops during the War. Once materials became available, dads throughout the country set about making all kinds of toys to satisfy the demands of the post-war baby boom. The fretwork side of the business gradually returned to pre-war levels, and the

Above: Capstan and turret lathe operators Beryl Moy (foreground, left), Bertie Wilson (foreground, right)

Left: Harry Tooke making a brake screw for a 40 ton trailer on a centre lathe

Below: Margaret Long machines a small chuck for the Hobbies Simplex fretwork hand drill on a Ward No. 2A capstan lathe

retail division had great difficulty in keeping up with demand. The Annual Handbook was restored to a page content of 120 pages with a corresponding price rise to 1/6. Only three treadle fretmachines were offered after the War - the A1, Gem and the Hobbies Bicycle Fretmachine, which was advertised as being suitable for occupational therapy and many were sold to hospitals to be used for that purpose. The motor-driven Marvel bench top machine was also available, and two lathes, the Companion, which had been in production since the days of

J. H. Skinner & Co., and a bench top model. Projects quickly switched from war themes to the more mundane models of caravans, tramcars, garages, forts and doll's houses, etc.

The engineering division, however, did not enjoy the same good fortune. A contract had been obtained from an Essex firm for making chaff cutters and grinding mills which were destined for backward African countries. These had to be made

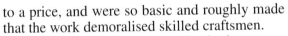

Above: Finishing chaff cutters and grinding mills for export to Africa

Left: Alan Baker operates a capstan lathe

Below (left): Phylis Arthurton shows her skills on another capstan lathe

Below (right): Leslie Downing making aircraft bomb carrier adapter plates on a Rhodes 120 ton press (with safety guard removed for the photograph)

to a price, and were so basic and roughly made that the work demoralised skilled craftsmen.

They were further demoralised when some ministry work was sub-contracted to Wright Engineering in another part of the town. Bomb-heads were taking skilled turners at Hobbies seven hours to produce on old lathes, which had been

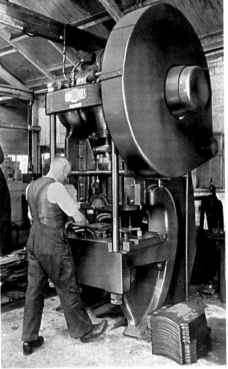

installed before the First World War. Wright Engineering had installed modern copy lathes which could turn out a bomb-head in 20 minutes, and only required unskilled labour to operate. Moreover, the same labourer could operate three lathes, bringing the time element down from seven hours to seven minutes.

In February 1947, strikes by power workers caused considerable disruption and 90 employees at Hobbies had to be stood off. An emergency generator was brought in, and it was hoped to keep the rest of the 600 employees at work.

Above: Arthur "Risho" Williamson and Mrs. Sizeland operate 10 ton power presses

Left: Multi-spindle high speed drill operators, Ivy Head is third from left, second row

Below: 28 inch Archdale horizontal milling machine operators include Joyce Smith (3rd in 1st row), Eileen Valentine (1st in 2nd row) and Charlie Elliott (3rd in 2nd row)

GOLDEN JUBILEE CELEBRATIONS

The great event of post war years was the celebration of Hobbies' Golden Jubilee in October 1947. The introduction to the commemorative booklet, published to celebrate the 50 year jubilee, stated: "Greatness must start from small beginnings - in 1897 it was only hoped that Hobbies would become a household word. Today that has been achieved.

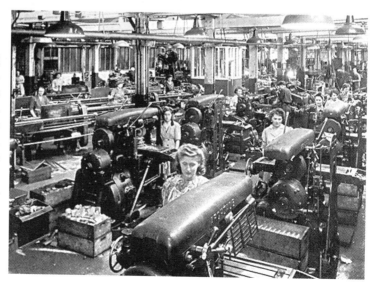

Progress has been maintained steadily through fifty years, and we see no reason why it should not continue for another fifty."

On 22nd October 1947, all the managers of Hobbies branches, departmental heads and the directors resumed their periodical visits to Head Office, which had been interrupted by the War. A tour of the factory, mills and offices (then standing on six acres of land)

was undertaken to show the visitors the wide variety of machinery and plant used to manufacture the wide range of Hobbies' products, from huge bomb carriers to tiny fretsaw blades. One was 17 ft. long, weighed half a ton, and contained 2,700 parts - the other was 5 in. long and 7 dozen were needed to weigh half an ounce!

The ubiquitous tiny blade was one of the products which made Hobbies a household

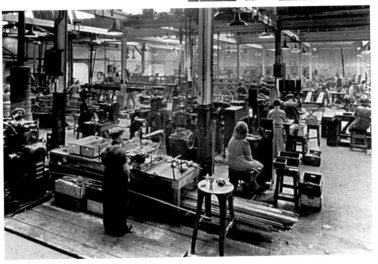

Top: 18 inch Archdale vertical milling machines in 1945 - left to right, Margaret Lister, Charlie Elliott (chargehand), Eileen Valentine

Centre: Assembling hand fretsaws - left to right, Ted Whitney, Ivy Cox, Beryl Burton, Pat Webster

Bottom: View of assembly shop, Harry Tooke in foreground

Hobbies' staff rush for the cycle sheds at the end of the day's work in 1945

name throughout the world. One hundredweight of special steel would make 900 gross of blades - 129,600! James Youngman, who had been with the firm a total of over 48 years, was in charge of the fretsaw blade making shop from 1927, and responsible for the manufacture of 8 - 9 million blades each year. Seven processes were required in their manufacture. The blades started life as sheet metal, which was cut into 6 in. lengths, then compressed into "planks", followed by tooth

Above: Joan Twiddy operates a bomb carrier adapter plate test rig

Right: Drawing office staff. Left to right, Joan Twiddy (inspector), Trevor Betts, Don Twiddy (chief inspector), Jean Barlow, ——, Yvonne Laws, Brian Betts, John Rickwood (foreground)

Left: Operating this test rig in 1945 are, left to right, Doreen Blades, Ruby Locke, Mitzi ——.

milling, shearing, hardening, tempering and inspection.

Elsewhere in the engineering department castings could be made up to 4 cwt, whilst in the saw mills huge bandsaws could handle timber up to 6 ft. in diameter and 18 ft. long. There were also important support departments such as drawing office, inspection section and packing department. The latter had to handle orders from the Tropics to Iceland and be able to ensure that goods would arrive in good condition, wherever the destination.

An exhibition of the firm's products was staged in the Memorial Hall in Norwich Street, and the evening was spent by the visitors discussing the details of export, wholesale, retail and mail order business in those days of restriction and frustrations.

The following day a lunch was given by the directors at the King's Head Hotel, in Norwich Street, at which all the directors, departmental heads and branch managers were present. The Chairman, Mr. Richard Jewson, welcomed those present and reported on the continued progress of the firm, and the various fretwork goods for which it had become a household name.

Mr. Jewson then spoke most warmly of the unfailing services Mr. Charles Bloxham had rendered since he joined the company 50 years previous, when he served at the original London Office in Paternoster Square.

A very handsome $12\frac{1}{2}$ ins. embossed silver salver was presented to Mr. Bloxham. It was engraved: "Presented by the Directors of Hobbies Limited to Charles R. Bloxham (London Manager and Branches Inspector) on his retirement after 50 years of loyal and devoted service, 1897-1947."

During his half century of service, Charles Bloxham had been responsible for arranging and controlling Hobbies' Stands at the British Industries Fair, and the Ideal Home, Model Engineer,

Hobbies' testing department in 1945. The second from front is Joan Twiddy; third from front is Edith Ruddock

93

Testing department 1945. 1st in right row, Emmie Smith; 1st in centre row, Miss Secker; 2nd in left row, Iris Long; Joan and Don Twiddy centre back

Schoolboys' and similar Exhibitions. He had undertaken six trips to Canada prior to the Hobbies Store being opened there in 1924. He had been responsible for branch replacement when enemy action destroyed those in Bishopgate and Newington Butts (London), Birmingham, and Hull (twice). During his service the turnover of the Branches had increased 700% in 30 years.

Mr. Bloxham was also presented with a handsome case of pipes and a pigskin pouch, with engraved initials, filled with cigarettes and tobacco, by Mr. N. B. Baker on behalf of the managers and staff of the various branches. Mr. Baker, as senior manager, had already supported Mr. Bloxham over a number of years, and was appointed as his successor.

In his speech Charles Bloxham expressed his gratitude for the gifts he had received, and spoke with emotion of the happy times he had had, and of the kindness shown to him.

At a little informal gathering later, a further presentation was made by Mr. H. Wagg on behalf of the senior members of the Head Office Staff at Dereham. It consisted of a handsome filled cigarette casket and table lighter.

Left to right, G. W. Firman (engineering progress department), A. L. Parkinson (chief inspector), E. Secker (foundry foreman)

THANKSGIVING SERVICE

Nearly a year later, the Chairman of the Board of Directors, Mr. Richard Jewson, suggested arrangements should be made for a church service to express thanks for the preservation of personnel and works from enemy attack during the recent war. So on Wednesday 22nd September, a Thanksgiving Jubilee Service was held in Dereham Parish Church. Although the church had a capacity of over 1,200, there were large numbers who could not get seats but had to stand at the back of the church and in the porch. The service was conducted by the Vicar, the Rev. Noel Boston, MA, FSA, and ministers of the other denominations took part. The Rev. T. Thompson led the prayers, and a reading was given by Senior-Capt. R. Ambrose (Salvation Army). The band of the Dereham Branch British Legion accompanied the singing, which was led by a mixed choir of works employees. The directors were present, as well as members of the Urban and Rural District Councils. The Vicar delivered an inspiring and appropriate address in which he stressed the need for the spirit of the service, that the fruits of the sacrifice of those who had laid down their lives in the war should not be wasted.

After the service, the whole company went to the Vicarage meadow, where an enormous marquee had been erected so that nearly 900 employees of

Above: Assembling the "Gem" fretmachine in 1945

Left: Working on the electrical wiring system on 8,000 lb. bomb carriers, Horace Mack in trilby, top left, and behind him, Jimmy Head. Iris Steward left foreground

Below: Light engineering assembly shop. Included in the picture are Nibby Webster, Liz Everett, Gay Head, Joan Harbour, Lou Brooks, Nelly Rudd, Joyce Nobbs, Horace Mack, Ivy Chambers

the firm, and families and friends, could sit down to tea. Because the Chairman, Mr. Richard Jewson, was ill, his brother, Mr. Frank Jewson, made a speech on his behalf. He expressed the hope that "something of the same kind may happen in another 50 years". He added, "Throughout the whole of the

Five of the 1947 Board of directors: left Richard Jewson (chairman); right, Edward C. A. Green (managing director); below left, Major Arthur R. Pratt; centre, Frank Jewson (vice-chairman); below right, Bertrand Wm. Jermyn

James Hanly, Kenneth Jewson and William Lawrence Fisher, pictured on page 83, were also directors

firm's existence the directors had had the loyal unswerving support of the employees and without it the firm would not then have been in existence. The continuance of Government contracts after the war testified to the quality of work which had been done by all employees". There were then three cheers for the Chairman, who, despite his illness, had made a long journey to be present.

On behalf of the employees and pensioners of the firm, a number of whom were present, Mr. M. R. Moore, assistant engineer, thanked the directors for their generous and enjoyable effort, and this was received with loud applause. Afterwards a Punch and Judy Show was put on for the children, and an all-round BBC entertainer, Bert Bradshaw, provided entertainment for the adults. The British Legion Band rendered several musical items during the evening.

SAD NEWS ARRIVES

Following the celebrations of 1947 and 1948, several bereavements were to sadden all associated with Hobbies. At the beginning of January 1949, news reached Dereham that the founder and first managing director of Hobbies, John Henry Skinner, had died on Christmas Eve, 1948. John Skinner was in his 89th year and was visiting his son in South Africa for Christmas. With failing sight, he had opened a door not knowing where it led. Unfortunately it led to a cellar, and John Skinner stumbled and fell down the steps and died as a result of his injuries. His substantial involvement in the establishment and success of Hobbies has been documented in foregoing pages; although he had not been involved

*Right: Exhibition of Hobbies'
products held in the Memorial Hall,
Dereham, as part of the 1947 Jubilee
celebrations - Mr. Trappett (2nd from
left) talks to visitors*

in the running of the firm for over 40 years, he had remained a shareholder, often attending annual meetings, when he stayed at the King's Arms, Dereham.

On 16th February 1949, due to ill health, Mr. Richard Jewson resigned the chairmanship, and Frank Jewson resigned as vice-chairman. Mr. Edward Charles Annison Green was appointed

*Left: Some of the drawing office staff take a break
in 1947. Left to right, Brian Betts, Yvonne Laws,
John Rickwood, Bob Mantripp, Basil Day*

chairman and managing director and Major Arthur Pratt joint managing director. James Hanly was appointed deputy chairman.

Frank Jewson died on 27th March 1949. His death was followed on 16th June 1949, by that of his brother, Mr. Richard Jewson.

He had been a director of Hobbies for 42 years, many early years as vice-chairman, and chairman for 28 years. He was a keen tennis player and had played until he was 80. He was founder member of Eaton Lawn Tennis Association and was captain at one time. He was twice president of Norfolk

Hobbies' lorry is loaded in 1947

The Directors, Branch and Departmental Managers pictured on the occasion of their visit to Dereham on 22nd October 1947.

Left to right, back row: N. B. Baker (New Oxford Street), H. Wagg (Buyer and Supply Manager), A. H Parker (Glasgow), K. S. Jewson (Engineering director), L. K. Kennard (Leeds), W. A. Clarke (Sales manager), S. W. Chambers (Chief draughtsman).

Centre row: H. Redstone (Birmingham), F. C. Reeve (Old Broad Street), D. Browning (Southampton), W. F. Chambers (Editor "Hobbies Weekly" and publicity manager), G. H. Wilkin (Sheffield), W. B. Cummings (Manchester), R. H. Mason (Hull), K. A. Field (Technical and engineering draughtsman).

Front row: J. R. Johnson (Saw mills manager), S. R. Rudd (Secretary), Mrs. H. Redstone (Birmingham), C. R. Bloxham (Supt. manager and branches inspector), E. C. A. Green (Managing director), E. C. Clark (Walworth Road), R. K. Moore (Assistant engineer)

Lawn Tennis Association and represented the County. Richard Jewson was also a keen golfer, and was credited with suggesting the formation of Norwich Golf Club. He left £77,321 gross, and on Monday 20th June, Hobbies' works and offices were closed for the day of his funeral as a mark of the high respect in which he was held.

On 28th August 1949, two new directors were appointed to the board: John Howlett Jewson, timber merchant of Mergate Hall, Bracon Ash, Norwich, and Frank Beverley Jewson, solicitor of 8 Branksome Close, Norwich.

During 1949, the publicity manager and editor of *Hobbies Weekly*, William Chambers, retired. Having been a journalist on the Yarmouth Independent, then editor of *Hobbies Weekly* for nearly thirty years, he decided to have a change in direction in his retirement. So he purchased Harry Webster's newsagents business in the Market Place, and started selling newspapers rather than writing the news! He was succeeded by James A. Wordingham.

11

The Lull Before The Storm

IN the early 50s, the circulation of *Hobbies Weekly* had risen to 75,000 copies per week, and the *Hobbies Handbook* sold 175,000 copies per year, and both were read in 50 countries. There was little indication of the difficulties to come, although problems with industrial relations were beginning to manifest themselves, something which had previously been quite rare at Hobbies. On 19th March 1951, the authorised capital of Hobbies was increased to £120,000 by the creation of 50,000 ordinary shares at £1 each. On 8th March 1954 the authorised capital was again increased to £170,000 by the creation of another 50,000 ordinary shares at £1 each.

The tractor, used to haul timber from Hobbies' meadow in Swanton Road in 1950, is driven by Jimmy Kirk, centre Fred Secker, right Nobby Clarke

Hobbies 'A' team, winners of the Dereham Table Tennis League, season 1950-51, receiving their trophies after the final in the Memorial Hall, Dereham, from Mrs. Dreibholtz. Left to right: Bob Mantripp, Basil Day, Ivor Vincent, Joe Allen, Leslie Potter (captain) and John Clarke (partly hidden)

Post-war inflation took the price of Hobbies Handbook to 2/-, and the 1953 issue kept the modeller right up to date by offering plans for the Coronation Chair and Coronation Coach (although these had been resurrected from previous coronation issues), Britain's first jet bomber, the Canberra, and the Bristol Brabazon, which was used on the London-New York route. These were published alongside evergreens which had been in every Handbook since the first issue, such as picture frames, handkerchief boxes, firescreens, and the model of St. Paul's Cathedral, which was given away as an inducement to subscribe to the first volume of Hobbies Weekly. The 1954 issue contained

a set of cut-out pictures of football stars of the time: Trevor Ford (Sunderland), Billy Wright (Wolves), Jack Froggatt (Portsmouth), Roy Bentley (Chelsea), Nat Lofthouse (Bolton), Jimmie Logie (Arsenal), Ted Ditchburn (Spurs), and Jack Milburn (Newcastle) - most totally unknown to many football fans today!

DEPARTURES AND ARRIVALS

At the end of April 1954, Horace Wagg retired at the age of 73. He had been born in Docking and originally worked in the grocery trade before joining

Hobbies in 1901. After a few months at Dereham, he went to work at what was then the company's Head Office in Paternoster Square, where he was departmental manager. Horace Wagg returned to Dereham in 1908 to take charge of the general supply and distribution department, a post he occupied

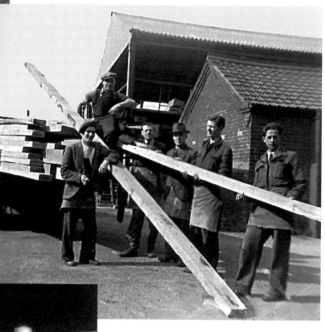

Top: Left to right, Lottie Brown, Gladys Boast, and Betty Firmin take a break from the woodwork department in 1950

Above: Unloading imported timber in 1952: 3rd from left Joe Allen, 4th from left Cecil Johnson, 5th from left Ted Barty

Left: Woodwork department employees pose for the camera in 1951. Extreme right back row, Nelson Secker; Front row, left to right, ——, George Brown, Bettie Brown, Gladys Boast, Arthur Gould

for 46 years. Mr. Wagg was succeeded by Mr. A. I. Stroulger, aged 37, who had returned to Dereham from the Manchester Retail Branch.

Towards the end of 1954, William Scales, previously a sub-editor with the Norwich Mercury Series for six years, was appointed advertising and publicity manager. He succeeded James A. Wordingham, who left after four years to join the publicity department of Bakelite Ltd. in London. Bill Scale's duties also included editorial control of *Hobbies Weekly* and *Hobbies Handbook*.

The authorised capital of the firm was once again increased to £220,000 on 4th April 1955 by the issue of another 50,000 ordinary shares at £1 each.

On 1st August 1955, another long-serving stalwart died. Mr. Edward Charles Annison Green died just before his 81st birthday. He had joined Hobbies at the end of the 1890s, just before the South African War. He had been responsible for opening branches in Liverpool, Birmingham, Manchester and Leeds. He was appointed company secretary

A Royal Visit to the Hobbies stand at the British Industries Fair at Olympia in 1953. Left to right: Miss E. Meadows, the present Duke of Gloucester, the late Prince William of Gloucester, William Clarke (sales manager), Princess Alice Duchess of Gloucester

Working on bomb cone heads in the late 1950s. Left to right: Janet Bower, Dougie Webster (charge-hand), Edie Page, Flo Johnson, Janet Webster, Heather Hill, Maureen Walpole, —

and manager in 1907, a director in 1917, managing director in 1928 and chairman in 1949. Edward Green was closely associated with the Cowper Congregational Church, where he was a life deacon, and had been church treasurer from 1915 to 1945. He had also been a keen tennis player and had played until after his 80th birthday.

James Laffan Hanly, of 1 Eaton Road, Eaton, Norwich, was appointed to succeed Edward Green as chairman and Major Arthur Reginald Pratt, of Billingford Lodge, Dereham, was appointed deputy chairman and managing director.

One of the most popular kits in the mid-50s was initiated by the trends in the popular music of the time—rock and roll and skiffle had made their appearance, and "assemble-it-yourself" guitar kits were extremely good sellers to the budding Bill Haley and Lonnie Donegan.

At Christmas, 1956, a new branch was opened in Newcastle-on-Tyne and Derek White left Dereham to become the first manager of the branch.

In May 1957, the branch managers made their periodical visit to Head Office at Dereham. They were joined by the managers of the various departments and entertained to lunch by the directors. Mr. J. L. Hanly (chairman) welcomed the visitors and after lunch the party, led by Major A. R. Pratt (managing director) and Mr. W. L. Fisher (engineering director), toured the factory and saw mills to see new products and equipment.

DIAMOND JUBILEE REACHED

The Annual General Meeting, held on 25th November 1957, marked the Diamond Jubilee of Hobbies. At the time this milestone was reached the firm had 13 branch shops and a turnover of £750,000. The number employed had dropped to 500 people, and the weekly circulation of *Hobbies Weekly* had dropped to 60,000 copies. Lunch was given after the meeting for the directors and shareholders, many of whom had been associated with Hobbies since the earliest days. Among them were Rev. Conrad A. Skinner (son of the founder, John Henry Skinner), Bert and Conrad Jermyn (sons of Sir Alfred Jermyn, who succeeded John Henry Skinner as managing director), and the third generation was represented by Mr. Edward Jermyn. Also present were Col. J. H. Jewson and Miss M. Jewson (son and daughter of Richard Jewson, third chairman). Other members of the Jewson family were also present, including Mr. K. S. Jewson (one of the directors at that time), and Mr. Beverley Jewson (son of the former vice-chairman, Frank Jewson). Also present was Mr. John Green (nephew of Mr. E. C. A. Green, who succeeded Richard Jewson as chairman and was connected with the firm for 50 years), and Mr. H. W. Fox, who was one of the oldest shareholders.

One of the directors, Bertrand William Jermyn, of 161 Wootton Road, King's Lynn, died on 4th January 1958.

Frederick J. Cann, originator of the "Practical" magazines died in his sixties on 19th February 1959, just after another of his brainchilds, the Practical Householder Exhibition, opened at Earls Court. He was a scientist, engineer and watchmaker, and had written 200 books. He had become editor of *Hobbies Weekly* in 1930 at £8 per week. His brother, Sir

Branch and Departmental managers visit the sawmill in 1957. Front row, extreme right, Willam Fisher, 2nd from right Major Pratt, 4th from right C. Mackrell; back row, extreme right, A. I. Stroulger

Sydney Cann, designed the Hurricane when he worked for Hawker Aircraft. Frederick Cann was responsible for bringing out Practical Wireless, Practical Mechanics, Practical Television, Practical Motorist and Motorcyclist, and Practical Householder. The last was the most popular and there cannot be many contemporaries who do not remember at least one of the titles with nostalgia.

By the end of 1959 Hobbies had opened another retail shop - The Model Aircraft Shop (Hobbies) Ltd., Queen's Buildings, Roof Gardens, Central London Airport, Hounslow, Middlesex, more familiar today as London Heathrow. However, by 1963, this branch had ceased to operate.

HOBBIES SAIL A STRAIGHT COURSE

In March 1960, Hobbies produced and marketed "The Flying Cat", a full size catamaran designed by F. M. & J. A. Montgomery of Sark, Channel Islands. The catamaran was 16 ft. long with a beam of 7 ft. 6 ins. and a draught of 7 ins. It carried 200 square feet of sails and weighed 235 lb. The price (without sails) was £254. Prototypes were sent to America and Canada for trials and evaluation, and locally trials and demonstrations were carried out at Lowestoft and Oulton Broad. In late March the catamaran was sailed across the Channel for its first series of races at Boulogne, and was placed second overall. Later in the year, following the success of the catamaran, a dinghy kit was "launched". This was designed to accommodate one adult plus one child, but, to prove the dinghy's safety and buoyancy, in November it was demonstrated for the press by three adults, John Randall, Bill Scales (editor of *Hobbies Weekly*) and D. Rayner - on the Neatherd Pond!

This aerial view of Hobbies' factory was photographed in the early 50s by the late George Ernest Swain. The wasteland behind the factory was once John Green's nursery, later Hobbies' horticultural department. The whole site is now occupied by the Somerfield supermarket.

Encouraged by the success of their catamaran and dinghy kits, Hobbies unveiled their 11 ft. single seat, canvas-skinned canoe kit, the PBK10, which had been designed by P. W. Blandford. This made its debut on Hobbies' Stand at the 1960 Daily Express Boat Show, held at Earls Court. This was quickly joined by the PBK14, a 14 ft tourer, the PBK15, a similar sized fast tourer, the PBK20, a two-seater, popular with scouts and youth clubs. These were all designed by P. W. Blandford, as were the PBK16, a rigid plywood-skinned, flat-bottomed dinghy, and the PBK 24, a single seat folding canoe which was advertised as "the only canoe which packs into one bag small enough to go on a bus"!

George Brooks (left) and Alan Marsham working on bomb cone heads in 1959

AN IMPRESSIVE SERVICE RECORD

On the last day of the decade Sidney Remington Rudd retired at the age of 73 after 60 years service - an impressive record. He had been company secretary since July 1945 following 3 years as assistant secretary. Prior to 1942 he had been the firm's accountant in charge of Head Office. He originally joined Hobbies on 1st January 1901 as a clerk in the Horticultural Department at the age of $13\frac{1}{2}$ years on the recommendation of his headmaster, Mr. H. J. Barnaby. When

Retirement of Hobbies' company secretary, S. R. Rudd on 31st December 1960 - left to right, Major Pratt, S. R. Rudd, G. W. Wilkin (London area manager), A. I. Stroulger (supply manager), W. Scales (Editor "Hobbies Weekly"), C. Mackrell (chief draughtsman)

young Sidney Rudd first joined the Horticultural Department he worked under John Green in the nursery office, which used to be almost opposite the Memorial Hall in Norwich Street, Dereham. He subsequently rose to become head clerk in that department, but the outbreak of the First World War halted all work in the Horticultural Department and he was transferred to work in the engineering and woodwork departments.

In 1915 Sidney Rudd joined the 6th Suffolk Cyclists and served in France. He was wounded at Arras and sent home in September 1916, only to return to the front early the following

Assembling and testing fretwork drills - left to right, Miss S. Howlett, Miss E. Page, Miss M. Chambers, Miss M. Drew, Miss M. Morris and Miss J. Chaney

year. After demob from the army he resumed his career with Hobbies as manager of Head Office. During the Second World War he was the firm's accountant and chief executive and responsible for dealing with the increased pressure of work brought about by the war and Government contracts and severe limitations in staffing.

Sidney Rudd was succeeded as company secretary by Mr. Gerard Michael Master, who was previously employed by the Kenning Motor Group. Also retiring on the same day was Kenneth Scott Jewson.

On 4th December 1961, the issue of 20,000 ordinary shares at £1 each increased the authorised capital of Hobbies to £240,000.

At the end of the year, Horace Wagg, then aged 80, and his wife Ellen, aged 84, died within 5 days of each other. They lived at 45 Bradgate Villas, Crown Road, Dereham, and

Packing fretwork kits in the mid-1950s are, nearest the camera, Mrs. S. West and Mrs. M. A. Reeve

Horace had joined Hobbies in 1901, becoming departmental manager of the London Office. He returned to Dereham in 1908 to become Supply Manager, a post he held for over 45 years until his retirement in 1953.

In January 1962 the AEU was in dispute with employers over pay rates, and a one day token strike was called on 5th February. Leslie Potter, district secretary of the AEU, confirmed, in a statement to the press, that there had been a 100% response to the strike call. The post-war labour market was in no mood to return to pre-war conditions of employment where the employer called the tune and workers had to be grateful they had a job. They thought that the post-war boom should be equally shared between employer and worker, and there had been frequent confrontations involving rates of pay, conditions or holidays.

HOBBIES PROFIT FROM ERROR

In October 1962, Hobbies made the headlines in the local and national press, and received television coverage, due to a sheet of six stamps! It appears that a girl in the office was looking for a pair of scissors to cut up a sheet of six halfpenny stamps, three of which were unperforated. They had been sent in by a customer as part payment for goods. The young lady was advised to show them to Bill Scales, who was an authority on philately. Bill Scales recognised their rarity and potential value. Eventually the stamps were sold in London for £150 - and management decided that the money would be used to "help defray the increased cost of printing *Hobbies Weekly*"! No doubt this decision was somewhat unpopular among the staff!

In November 1962, Leslie Potter had aspirations to become a Member of Parliament and was chosen as prospective Labour candidate for Hunting-donshire. He had been successful in trade union circles, being then a member of the AEU National

Sawing planks on one of Hobbies' large bandsaws in 1960, left to right, Malcolm Jarrett, ———, Ernie Large

Committee, and in local government, having previously served as a member of Norfolk County Council, and a member of Dereham Urban District Council for eleven years. At the General Election of 1964, a Conservative government was returned for their fifth term in office. Leslie Potter was not elected, coming second to the Tory candidate, the Rt. Hon. David Lockhart-Mure Renton (now Lord Renton), who polled 20,320 votes to Leslie Potter's 12,456. The seat subsequently, of course, became that of John Major, who was destined to become Prime Minister.

On 3rd December 1962, the 66th Annual General Meeting was held at the Maid's Head Hotel, Norwich. Attending were James Hanly JP (chairman), Major A. R. Pratt (deputy chairman and joint managing director), W. L. Fisher (joint managing director) and directors, Col. J. H. Jewson, F. B. Jewson, and J. E. Green. The trading profit of £36,361 for the year was announced. By the 67th Annual General Meeting, held at the same place on 2nd December 1963, profit for the year had increased to £45,356. However, by then it was apparent that all was not well with Hobbies. The Government's "stop-go" attitude towards defence resulted in a loss of work to the firm, both directly and indirectly. An important customer, Microcell of Blackwater, Hampshire, announced that it was to cease manufacturing defence weapons due to "the unreliability of the market". Microcell had made a loss of £465,000 in 1962.

Packing goods in the supply department for the branches and agents in 1959 are, left to right, Joyce Matthews, George Large, and Len Titmus

Labour problems continued to disrupt, both nationally and locally. At the Blackpool Conference of the AEU in May 1963, Leslie Potter moved a resolution for the introduction of a third week's holiday, claiming: "With increasing pressure on the workers due to new methods and techniques in industry, it is clear that there is not only an increase in productivity, but an increase in the number of workers whose health is failing because of the growing pressure".

On 2nd December 1963, Mr. Gerard Master, the company secretary, was appointed a director of the company. He joined a board of directors who were reaching their senior years; none had successors following them into the firm. Trade was falling away at a rapid rate, the number of employees had been reduced, and investment in up-to-date machinery was badly needed. Although most were probably not aware of the fact at the time, the decline was gaining momentum at a rate which was going to be difficult to check.

HOBBIES TAKEN OVER

At the end of July 1964, when most of the 428 employees were on their annual two week's holiday, the fears of many were confirmed when it was announced that a take-over bid had been made by Industrial and Commercial Holdings Ltd., a large London based concern. Among the many companies owned by Industrial and Commercial Holdings Ltd. was the Guiterman Group of toy makers, whose products it was intended to sell through the Hobbies retail outlets and mail order organisation. The offer was for 28/- for £1 ordinary shares and at par for £1 preference shares, making the bid worth £328,000. The Hobbies board of directors recommended acceptance of the offer. The chairman, Mr. James Hanly announced that if the bid was successful only two of the present board would be retained, Mr. W. L. Fisher (joint managing director) and Mr. Gerard Master (company secretary). Those to be retired were Mr. James Hanly, Major A. R. Pratt (joint managing director), Col. J. H. Jewson, Mr. F. Beverley Jewson, and Mr. John E. Green.

In an interview with the local press, Mr. Hanly said, "there is a lot of sentiment attached to this old company, and none of us is overjoyed by this thing in a way, but it is for the benefit of the firm and we have to think of that. We live in the days of bigger units. There would probably be more emphasis on toys, and new lines were likely to be introduced at the Dereham Works".

A notice was posted in the works informing the few workers who were carrying out maintenance work, and the rest of the employees when they returned after their holiday, that Mr. Julius Trup, chairman of the Guiterman Group intended to develop the company further than Hobbies had been able to do with their limited resources and that the firm would continue to trade as Hobbies Ltd., and all pension and other rights would be preserved.

A postal strike at the time held up the take-over bid for a while, as offers did not reach shareholders in time for them to register their acceptance. However, by the third week of August, Industrial and Commercial Holdings Ltd. had received acceptance of their offer from 90% of the shareholders, but the original closing date of 20th August 1964 was extended to 15th October 1964, mainly to accommodate shareholders living abroad. Nevertheless, Industrial and Commercial Holdings Ltd. declared the offer was unconditional and that they were likely to complete the take-over long before that date.

At an Extraordinary General Meeting held at Head Office on 21st August 1964, the resolution was passed enabling Industrial and Commercial Holdings Limited to acquire the whole of the issued share capital of the Company, and to make

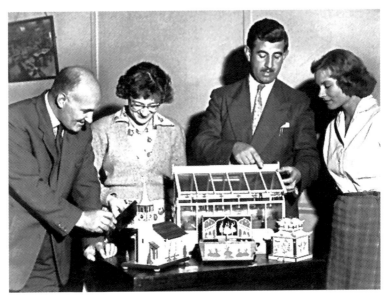

Admiring new items in the 1960 Handbook are, left to right, Bill Scales (editor of Hobbies Weekly), ———, Cecil Mackrell (chief draughtsman), and Elizabeth Pratt (Major Pratt's daughter)

payments to directors as compensation for loss of office. The compensation amounted to £7,000 to Major A. R. Pratt, and £1,400 to be divided between Mr. J. L. Hanly, Col. J. H. Jewson, Mr. F. W. B. Jewson and Mr. J. E. Green.

THE NEW BROOM SWEEPS CLEAN

On 23rd September 1964, Major Pratt retired after 41 years service. He received from the combined Head Office, engineering and sawmill staff, a set of cut glass goblets and tumblers, which were presented by Mr. Gerard Master, company secretary. In his speech, Mr. Master said, "Everyone would have good cause to remember Major Pratt's kindness and readiness with which he always gave a helping hand". Major Pratt said that it was rather sad to be leaving a firm after 41 years, but they had been happy years and he was very grateful to everyone for their loyalty not only to him, but also to the firm.

Earlier in the day Major Pratt had been presented with fishing tackle and other gifts from the managers of Hobbies, including the Branch managers, also a piece of antique furniture from members of the old board of directors of Hobbies.

Major Pratt had been born in Lincolnshire, the son of a doctor, and served with the Indian Army for seven years before joining Hobbies in 1923. In 1926 he became company secretary and was made a director in 1938. With the outbreak of the Second World War, Major Pratt was recalled to the army and spent six years with the Royal Norfolk Regiment. After the war he returned to Hobbies and became joint managing director with special responsibility for marketing.

Presentation to Major Pratt, on his retirement, in 1964. Left to right, W. A. Clarke, S. R. Rudd, C. Mackrell, Major A. R. Pratt, G. Master, A. I. Stroulger, W. Scales, G. Wilkins and Miss Doris Hatton

Also retiring on the same day were James L. Hanly, John H. Jewson, F. Beverly Jewson and John Green, all having resigned from the board of directors as required by the terms of the take-over by Industrial and Commercial Holdings Limited. On the same date the following were appointed to form a new board with the existing directors, William Fisher and Gerard Master: Julius Trup of Norrice Lea, London; James Douglas Spooner of 25 Hyde Park Gardens, London; and Walter William Hunt of 19 Lambarde Road, Sevenoaks, Kent, and Hobbies reverted to a private company. The background of the three new directors was interesting. Julius Trup was director of 24 other firms, James Spooner had seven directorships and Walter Hunt had eight.

ENGINEERING WORKS IS FIRST CASUALTY

Industrial and Commercial Holdings Ltd. were only interested in the retail and mail order business, so they sold off the engineering works to Associated Veneer Panels. Because the retail side was to continue trading under Hobbies' name, the engineering business was renamed Dereham Engineering Ltd. Associated Veneer Panels had a track record of take-overs and closures - Dereham was to be no exception. After trading for a while the business was reduced even further and finally sold to Garrett of Leiston in February 1969. Garrett struggled along for a while but the firm closed down completely on 16th September 1977. The large site was sold to Norfolk Gardens, who had plans to develop it as a housing estate. However, after standing derelict for some years, the site was acquired by Keymarkets (later Gateway, now Somerfield) for development into what was then Dereham's biggest superstore.

Shortly after Industrial and Commercial Holdings Ltd. took over Hobbies, two more long serving stalwarts retired. The first to go, after 45 years service, on Saturday 2nd January 1965, was Mr. Gordon Baney. He was 65 years old and had started with Hobbies as an office boy in 1913. He served with 2nd Battalion Middlesex Regiment in France towards the end of the First World War and returned to Head Office at Dereham in 1920. For twenty years prior to his retirement, Gordon Baney had been in charge of the export department. He was presented with a clock from his colleagues.

On the following Monday, 4th January 1965, Mr. W. Clarke retired after completing 42 years service. He was born in Birmingham and became the first manager of the newly opened Brighton Branch in 1923. The following year he had the honour of being chosen to inaugurate and manage the Toronto Branch, a post he occupied until 1930 when he returned to Dereham. His colleagues presented him with a power drill and a heater, and the Branch managers gave him a garden sun shelter.

On 17th May 1965 another appointment was made to the board of directors, Mr. Lawrence Rose of 11 Fairacres, Roehampton Lane, London. He was also a director of four other firms. Appointed to the board at the same time was George Stanley Turnbull, an engineer of Lodge House, Bawburgh, Norwich, but he resigned on 30th November 1966.

THE DECLINE GATHERS MOMENTUM

The retail division struggled along under the new management. The "new broom" swept away old and proven methods and introduced new merchandise—which proved to be a total failure. The readership of *Hobbies Weekly* dwindled to less than 20,000 copies per week, making the magazine unprofitable, and it ceased publication by the end of 1965. The Hobbies Bicycle Fretmachine was also dropped in 1965, leaving the Gem and A1 the only treadle machines available.

For the year ended 30th June 1966 the company made a net trading profit of £11,324, plus profit on sale of fixed assets of £7,435 - a total of £18,759. In the same period of trading *Hobbies Weekly* made a trading loss of £617. Dereham Supply Branch made £9,023 loss but the Retail Branches made £13,520 profit, and the engineering department also made a profit of £6,176.

On 13th July 1966, Ivor Theodore St. Claire McCarthy, of Greytiles, Bittering Road, Gressenhall, a merchandising manager, was appointed to the board, but he ceased to be a director on 17th March 1967. His directorship was taken up by Alec H. Attwood of 34 Ryculf Square, Blackheath, London, who was appointed on 24th April 1967.

THE DEATH OF AN ENTITY

The worst fears of all Dereham people, particularly those associated with Hobbies, were realised in August 1968. An Extraordinary General Meeting of the firm, held at Lee House, London Wall, London, on 1st August, passed a special resolution to change the name of Hobbies to Exham Realisations Ltd. with effect from 8th August 1968.

Then, a resolution passed at a meeting of the company on 4th December 1968 decided the firm should be voluntarily wound up.

The company had been brought to its knees - the once great name of Hobbies, which had been known all over the world for over 70 years, came to an ignominious end. The liquidators appointed to deal with the winding up were Thomas John Lawrence Milner and John Hallett Gaston of Smallfield, Fitzhugh, Tillet & Co. of 24 Portland Place, London, W1 and Gillet House, 55 Basinghall Street, London, EC2.

The total assets at that time totalled £349,357 with liabilities of £19,212. The balance at the bank was £35,982 with £1,305 in hand.

On 31st December 1968, J. D. Spooner resigned as director, and on 21st February 1969 G. M. Master resigned as director and secretary. Three days later J. H. Gaston resigned as a liquidator. Julius Trup remained in office to oversee the final throes of the winding up procedures until 14th February 1973, when he too resigned. On 18th January 1977, a general meeting was held to receive a copy of the accounts to show how the property of the company had been disposed of and how the winding up process had been conducted.

The King of fretwork was dead - long live the King!

12

The Phoenix Rises

IVAN Stroulger was born at Bintree, Norfolk in 1916, during the First World War. In those days there were few leisure pursuits, and during the long winter evenings there was little for a young lad to do apart from reading and stamp collecting. It was then Ivan experienced his first contact with Hobbies, little knowing that half a century later he was to become responsible for perpetuating the name of Hobbies, not only in Dereham where the firm had started, but all over the world. Ivan had heard of the hobby of fretwork, which rather appealed to him, and asked for a fretwork set for Christmas. At Bintree school about half a dozen boys were able to take fretwork during the craft period on Friday afternoons. Ivan took the hobby seriously and continued into his teen years. He had *Hobbies Weekly* delivered every Wednesday from the local newsagent and visited Hobbies Supply Depot at Dereham for supplies of wood and fretsaw blades. In those days it was a twenty minute journey by train from Foulsham station, costing 10d. return. Later he purchased his first cycle, a Hercules, for £3.19.9, and gained independence from public transport.

Ivan and Margaret Stroulger on their wedding day, 14th September 1940

ARTISTIC TALENT NOT APPRECIATED BY HOBBIES

After leaving school Ivan worked for Langleys (later taken over by Cullen of Norwich), the local chemist, and became involved in serving customers, dispensing, window dressing, and any odd job required. Coming from an artistic family, Ivan had by then taken up sketching and painting; he even undertook the odd sign-writing job in the locality. The minister at the local Baptist Church, Rev. W. H. Wheele, was quite impressed with his work and took his latest effort to Norwich to show an artist friend, who was the daughter of Richard Jewson, a director of Hobbies. He thought there might be a vacancy in Hobbies' drawing office for a talented youngster. Unfortunately there was no vacancy, but when they heard Ivan was experienced in shop work they offered him a job in one of their London branches.

Ivan thought this was an opportunity not to be missed and accepted the offer. On 10th July 1936, at the age of 20, he started two weeks training at the Head Office in Dereham.

He spent the two weeks going round different departments to see how the business was run and how Hobbies' products were made. Then it was off to a new life in London. He managed to find lodgings through his friends in the Baptist Church and stayed with Rev. Wheele's mother at Barking in Essex, travelling to work by underground and working wherever he was required, but mainly at the Bishopgate and New Oxford Street branches.

After six months Ivan was offered a position as first assistant in the Manchester branch, replacing George Wilkin, who was returning to London. Ivan remembers travelling up to Manchester on the return half of his rail ticket, which was cheaper for Hobbies than purchasing two single tickets! Faced with finding suitable accommodation in a strange city, he contacted the minister of the local Baptist Church, who put him in touch with a congregation member, and he stayed for three years until he married in 1940. Ivan met his wife, Margaret Worrall, at Moss Side Baptist Church. The youngest of 10, Margaret had an earlier claim to fame when, as a child, she had the privilege of singing in the Manchester Children's Choir. Her voice was one of 250 recorded on 29th June 1929 singing "Nymphs and Shepherds", and this recording has since been reissued several times on different compilations and copies sold all over the world.

Ivan and Margaret Stroulger with their first-born, Alan, at Christmas 1942

Ivan remembers being involved in causing a traffic jam in Manchester shortly after his arrival! The manager of the Manchester branch, W. B. Cummings, decided to follow the lead of other branches and put on a display of fretwork in the large windows of the store. The manager operated a treadle fretsaw, Ivan used a hand frame at a bench, and the lad, Ken Jones, operated a lathe. So great was the interest in the display that huge crowds gathered outside and spilled out onto the road. The police were so concerned about the safety of the pedestrians, not to mention the obstruction to road users, that they had to ask the manager to call off the demonstration!

Between 1940 and 1946 Ivan served in the Forces and made his way up to Quartermaster Sergeant, returning after demobilisation to Manchester, where he and his wife set up home on the Benchill estate. He resumed his job at the Manchester branch of Hobbies, and, as well as serving as deputy branch manager, he acted as representative calling on Hobbies' agents in the area. He also attended major exhibitions, such as the British Industries Fair, and was responsible for setting up the Hobbies stand and dealing with the public during the fair.

A SPECIAL VISITOR

One day in August 1948, Ivan recalls a customer coming into Hobbies' Bull Ring Shop in Birmingham, when he was acting as relief holiday manager. The visitor was a well-tanned, dapper little man, very well dressed, wearing spats and carrying a Mallaca cane. It was John Henry Skinner, the founder of Hobbies Ltd.! They chatted for about half an hour. Ivan considered it a privilege to have met and spoken to the founder of Hobbies and often wonders what Skinner thought of the firm which he had left nearly half a century

Chalet Doll's House

previously. John Skinner died at the end of the year and it was probably one of the last visits he made to the firm he had created.

After the War, business was good for Hobbies, and quickly returned to pre-war levels. Ivan Stroulger was promised promotion back at Head Office in Dereham, but he had to wait patiently because there was a housing shortage. At last he was called to see Major Pratt, then Hobbies' Managing Director, and was offered the job of Buyer and

Supply Manager, to succeed Horace Wagg who was retiring after occupying the post since 1908. A company house in Elvin Road was part of the package. Ivan readily accepted the offer and moved back to Dereham during Coronation Week in June 1953. In his new job he was able

Gypsy Caravan Doll's House

Windmill Doll's House

to make valuable business contacts which stood him in good stead at a later date. Meanwhile the Stroulgers settled into a new life, and concentrated on raising their family of four sons, Alan, Philip, Geoffrey and Robert, all of whom had been born in Manchester. The family was later increased to five boys following the birth of John. In the early 60s Ivan travelled to many trade fairs, including the Nuremberg Trade Fair in Germany, which he attended annually with George Wilkin, then the London Manager, and the chap whom Ivan had replaced in Manchester!

The late 50s and early 60s represented a period of great change in the country. The privations of the war years were passing into history and people wanted a better life. Wages had risen to such levels that most workers could afford to take regular holidays, and buy luxuries such as the newly arrived television, perhaps a second-hand car and a wide range of toys for the children. The demand for Hobbies' products gradually declined, the company had failed to up-date their merchandise sufficiently to keep up with modern demands, and there were many other spare-time

*Pixie
Doll's
House*

occupations to attract all age groups. The directors of Hobbies were all approaching retirement age and none had heirs interested in entering the business. So the decision was made to sell the firm.

THE SHOCK OF REDUNDANCY

In March 1968, Ivan Stroulger was one of the many employees who were made redundant that year. To say this came as a shock is somewhat an understatement! At the age of 51, employment prospects were bleak. After a brief period trying to find another management position Ivan decided that the only way forward was to start his own business. He felt there was still a demand for well produced dolls' house kits, so he decided to design and make these from home in his garden shed. He was granted permission, by

East Dereham U.D.C., to use his home at 20 Elvin Road for that purpose for one year, and he went along to his solicitor to register the name of Dereham Handicraft Company on 7th May 1968. Ivan's redundancy money, amounting to just over £1,000, was invested in equipment and materials, and the production of ready-to-assemble doll's house kits commenced.

Garage

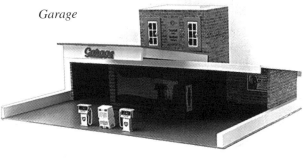

He introduced a range of six kits, a Pixie Doll's House, a Chalet Doll's House, a Gypsy Caravan Doll's House, a Windmill Doll's House, and for the boys, a model Garage and Fort Wyoming.

He was lucky, initially, that Hobbies were still trading and trying to clear large stocks. He was able to reach agreement with Mr. G. Master, the Managing Director at the time, to sell his kits through Hobbies' mail order facilities and was paid on a monthly basis.

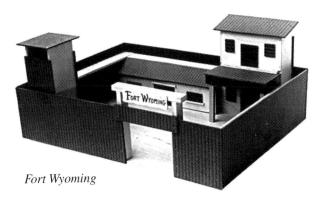

Fort Wyoming

Later that year, John Goddard, the Manager of the Dereham Branch of Barclays Bank, telephoned to ask if Ivan would be interested in taking a lease on the old Post Office garage and maintenance depot on the corner of Quebec Road and Swaffham Road, Dereham. This was coming up for auction, and John Goddard wanted to purchase the building for his nephew, at that time living in Scotland, who needed the building for the storage of his collection of vintage vehicles. He

The first Annual Handbook issued by Dereham Handicraft Company in 1975

would not need the premises for a few years, so was prepared to offer the building on a five year lease. At auction the premises were purchased by Goddard for £2,500. Ivan Stroulger took up the lease and in November 1968 moved in his production unit. He was still working on his own, with his wife part time in the office, which was registered at 20 Elvin Road. His eldest son Alan, who was a director with Aldiss of Fakenham, set up the book keeping and prepared the accounts for the auditor for the first year. Later his second eldest son, Philip, helped with cutting out, and was paid, as Ivan described, "a pittance".

When Hobbies finally ceased trading in 1969, Ivan had to look round for another outlet. He telephoned an old business acquaintance, Alan Hales, who operated a toy supply company in Leicestershire. Ivan Stroulger and his wife motored up to Hinkley for a meeting with Alan Hales, agreed terms and won a £15,000 order. Hales would supply all the packaging and Ivan the ready-to-assemble kits. The range was increased to eight, three were retained from the original range - Chalet Doll's House, Pixie Doll's House and the Garage. These were joined by three new doll's houses, the Manor, the Lynn and the Anglian, for the girls, and Castle Elvin and a Cavalry Fort for the boys. This arrangement appeared to be going well for the first year, but unfortunately the order was not repeated, as Hales' representatives were calling mainly on toy shops instead of DIY outlets, which would have brought in higher sales.

For a couple of years, Ivan Stroulger and Norman Lambert, who used to work in the drawing office at Hobbies, entered into a partnership and started a firm called "Hobby Trends" which was operated alongside Dereham Handicrafts Company. However this arrangement did not flourish and the partners went their separate ways. In 1975 Ivan Stroulger started a small mail order operation, and on 1st June 1975 changed the name of the firm to "Hobbies and Handicrafts (Dereham) Ltd."

LOGO BRINGS GOOD FORTUNE

Ivan always longed for the original Hobbies' trade mark to be assigned to him. He considered the familiar trade mark represented quality and reliability, and was recognised world wide. So, working on the old maxim, "nothing ventured, nothing gained", in late 1977 he wrote to the directors of the Guitermann Group and asked if

the old Hobbies' trade mark, together with patents and copyright ownership, could be transferred to him. To Ivan's amazement and immense pleasure he received a positive answer, and on 18th February 1978 he was assigned the familiar oval Hobbies' trademark.

Opening of the Hobbies' Museum and Craft Centre on 30th March 1993

Above: Robert Nicol, Mayor of Dereham (right), performs the opening ceremony with Robert Stroulger

Left: Founder of Hobbies (Dereham) Ltd., Ivan Stroulger, poses in the newly opened museum

Above: Ivan Stroulger (right) at the opening ceremony in 1993 with the last managing director of Hobbies Ltd., Mr. Gerard Master

That year was also the turning point in the fortunes of the company. Ivan realised that he needed to increase the circulation of his annual handbook, then running to 10,000 copies per year and sent by mail from Dereham. He contacted W. H. Smith (Wholesale) with a view to distribution through newsagents, but met with no joy. On the suggestion of Colin Chambers, who at that time ran a newsagents business in the Market Place, started originally by his father on his retirement from Hobbies as editor of *Hobbies Weekly*, Ivan contacted Moore Harness Ltd., a distributor in Leicestershire He was amazed to find that, years before, the magazine manager had been responsible for the distribution of 100,000 Hobbies' handbooks annually, when he worked for Horace Marshall Ltd.

Below: Shop assistant, Erika Toms, discusses the merits of the Regency doll's house with a prospective customer

(by then out of business)! They agreed terms and the print run was increased to 50,000 copies. Ivan wrote the articles and was responsible for all the artwork of the new handbook. When this was published, in August 1978, business quadrupled overnight and work had to go on late into the evenings.

On 10th September 1979 Ivan once again changed the name of the firm to "Hobbies (Dereham) Limited". The Phoenix had risen! Once again the famous brand name was trading from its original home town. A month later business was so good that Ivan's youngest son,

John, gave up his steady job at the Dereham accountants of Smith & Ludkin to join the firm. Soon Hobbies (Dereham) Ltd. were to take on their first employee, Norman White, who had sold his Newsagents business in Quebec Street and wanted a retirement job. One or two part-time employees were also taken on to cope with demand. The office still remained at the Stroulger's home in Elvin Road,

Above: Jenny Frost busy processing orders

Left: Christine Dunn, office manager, the first voice customers hear when they telephone Hobbies

Below: Justin Dack, warehouse manager, cutting parts for doll's house fittings

and daughters-in-law Barbara (Alan's wife) and Krystyna (Philip's wife) helped out part-time dealing with orders, correspondence and book-keeping. Even the grandchildren were pressed into service, acting as models for the front cover of the annual handbook!

In March 1987, Paul Larwood, who had been made redundant from his job with Bawdeswell Warehouses, joined the firm. He was a great asset as he was experienced in dealing with the mail order

side of the business and was able to introduce some useful contacts. He also turned his hand to helping John with the assembling of model kits. After ten years with Hobbies, Norman White retired in 1989.

EXPANSION LEADS TO MOVE

Business grew steadily every year until the firm began to outgrow their accommodation. At the end of 1989, the Central Woolgrowers building in Swaffham Road became available, and Ivan successfully negotiated for the premises. Although the buildings were almost derelict, and required considerable restoration, they were ideal for the company's purpose; even the racking left behind by the previous occupiers was able to be utilised. Hobbies (Dereham) Ltd. moved into their present home in the February of 1990. They had to put up with the building work going on

Assembling fittings for Hobbies' range of doll's house kits are Eileen Larwood (right, making windows) and Freda Rawling (below, making doors)

around them. On the 18th June that year, the second youngest of Ivan's son's, Robert, gave up his bank manager's job in Ilford to join the growing firm. After the main building work was completed, some of the outbuildings were turned into small craft units for start-up businesses. A small museum was created in another unit to display Hobbies'

John Stroulger, joint managing director, in the museum, which contains many of the fretmachines made by Hobbies over the years as well as several examples of the fretworker's craft. In the cabinet, left, is a fine model of the Coronation coach, and left foreground a model of St. Paul's Cathedral (see chapter 13)

memorabilia, which was being acquired by the company. This has proved to be an interesting attraction, both for ex-Hobbies employees and customers alike.

Later in 1990 Ivan decided to take a back seat and retired from management, leaving the firm in the capable hands of sons John and Robert, who became joint managing directors. Robert took on responsibility for the financial side of the business and business development, although the latter has now been taken on by Martin Flegg, who was recently appointed business development

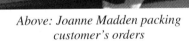

Above: Joanne Madden packing customer's orders

Left: Toby O'Brien filling paint pots

manager. John assumed responsibility for the manufacture of kits and the mail order side of the business.

In 1993, following completion of the restoration work, the premises were officially opened by Robert Nicol, then Mayor of Dereham Town Council, and many

Martin Flegg, business development manager, checks the design for Hobbies' "new baby", the Voyager radio-controlled yacht, launched in their 1999 handbook

ex-employees of Hobbies Ltd. attended the ceremony, including the last managing director of Hobbies, Mr. G. Master.

At the age of 82, Ivan Stroulger still maintains close contact with the firm, and takes responsibility for planning and making prototypes of the various projects which are featured each year in the annual catalogue.

In addition to the two directors, Hobbies (Dereham) Ltd. now employs six full-time and three part-time workers, and supplies a wide range of fretwork materials and equipment to customers country-wide and to most of the English speaking countries world-wide. Army personnel are still good customers, and orders usually stem from their involvement in world affairs in places like Germany, Northern Ireland and Bosnia. Orders are also received from most of the African Countries, Canada, Australia and New Zealand, even "odd" places like Sri Lanka and Iceland. Considering *Hobbies' Handbook* is distributed only in Australia outside the U.K., the wide spread of customers is quite surprising.

Some of the Hobbies "family" pictured outside the firm's retail shop at Dereham - left to right, Christine Dunn, Joanne Madden, Robert Stroulger, Ivan Stroulger, John Stroulger, Martin Flegg, Erika Toms, Freda Rawling, Justin Dack, Toby O'Brien

Ivan Stroulger (centre), founder of Hobbies (Dereham) Ltd. with sons John (left) and Robert, current joint managing directors

TRADITIONS MAINTAINED

The company still steadfastly maintains a policy of supplying traditional wooden kits, and each year they try to bring back something from Hobbies' past. Marquetry was reintroduced in 1993, Mamod steam engines in 1994. In 1997 yachts and boats based on original designs were revived, the yacht Venturesome and tug Plucky were joined by the Royal Yacht Britannia to commemorate its last year of regal service. This range is being enlarged to include newly designed yachts built on fibre glass hulls. Original designs for such items as clocks and musical boxes have been dusted down and given another airing, and in 1999 wooden aeroplanes are being reintroduced. Still available is a set of plans for building a model of St. Paul's Cathedral, which was given away from the very first issue of *Hobbies Weekly* if one subscribed to that journal! However, over half of the company's turnover is still derived from the sale of doll's house kits and accessories and traditional children's wheeled wooden toys. Many of these are being constructed by people who took up fretwork in

their teens, but are now making items for their grandchildren, even great-grandchildren, and who after sometimes sixty or seventy years are still loyal customers of Hobbies.

John Henry Skinner established his firm in the late 1880s, which was renamed Hobbies Limited in 1897. Apart from a brief hiccup, the words spoken at the Silver Jubilee, in 1947, were to be prophetic: "Greatness must start from small beginnings - in 1897 it was only hoped that Hobbies would become a household word. Today that has been achieved. Progress has been maintained steadily through fifty years, and we see no reason why it should not continue for another fifty ..."

The centenary has now been passed, and there seems no good reason why Hobbies should not continue to go from strength to strength for many more years to come!

Cover of the latest edition of Hobbies' Handbook

The Enthusiasts

THIS chapter has been included as a small tribute to the tens of thousands who have gained enjoyment over the years from articles published in *Hobbies Weekly* and the Hobbies' Annual Handbook, and from the products sold by Hobbies Ltd.

These fall mainly into three groups - fretwork, collecting and model making. Just one from each section has been featured as a representative of the many who have received much pleasure from their hobbies. They have not been included because they are regarded as the best in their fields, but simply because they are typical of the many enthusiasts who have in the past or still are enjoying a pleasant way of spending their spare time. They all, however, are connected in some way with the subject of this book, The Hobbies Story.

THE FRETWORKER

The first hobby featured is that on which Hobbies built their success - fretwork. Most fretworkers made dozens, if not hundreds of items, but the subject of this story has only made one piece; a replica of St. Paul's Cathedral!

Eric Barnes, of Sidcup, Kent, was appointed Vicar Choral at St. Paul's Cathedral in 1947. In 1949, when Second World War bomb damage was being repaired, he was able to retrieve a section of Wren's original oak beam as a souvenir. Eric retired in 1980, but the section of beam had lain forgotten in his garage until one day in 1993 when he decided to do something with it. He contacted Hobbies for a design sheet for a fretwork model of St.

Model of St. Paul's Cathedral on show in Hobbies' museum in 1998 - the remaining piece of oak beam in foreground

Paul's Cathedral. Eric Barnes had made the odd piece of furniture in the past, but had never tackled fretwork. Undaunted by his lack of experience, Eric painstakingly set about cutting the hard oak beam into thin sheets suitable for the model. Gradually it began to take shape, and working from morning till night on most days it took Eric over five months to complete his labour of love, and only a small piece of the beam remained. Then aged 79, Eric said he had a sense of urgency and was worried in case anything should happen. "It was my first model and it will be my last", he said. "My fingers get stiff now and I can't concentrate quite so much now, so I gave it my all".

Eric Barnes' model was exhibited at Sidcup Library in 1993, but most of the time it resides on his radio cabinet, a heirloom for his two daughters. Eric was pleased to exhibit the model at Hobbies' museum for the 1998 season, and many visitors made comments of admiration.

No doubt Eric did not realise the significance of a fretwork model of St. Paul's Cathedral in the history of Hobbies when he ordered the design. When *Hobbies Weekly* was first published on 19th October 1895, the free design given as an inducement to take out a subscription to the publication was ... a model of St. Paul's Cathedral! The original design, however, was for a model 32 inches long, and at some stage Hobbies reduced the scale by about 50%. Fortunately Eric's piece of oak beam was just sufficient for the smaller version! The design has been offered continuously by Hobbies since 1895, and is still featured in the latest 1999 Handbook.

Eric Barnes with his model of St. Paul's Cathedral made from part of an oak beam salvaged from repair work carried out on the original St. Paul's Cathedral

THE MODEL MAKER

The description "model maker" in this context is taken to mean someone who makes a smaller version of something which is absolutely true to scale and carries every detail of the original. When viewed without the benefit of a reference point which gives an indication of size, such as in a photograph, it is not possible to distinguish a model from the real thing.

Over the years Hobbies supplied raw materials, tools and detailed instructions to model makers for a myriad of models - ships, aeroplanes, locomotives, steam engines - the list goes on. But never once did it occur to Hobbies to include their own fretmachines for miniaturisation!

Alan Cambridge retired to Norfolk from his trade as a tool and gauge maker. With time on his hands, he decided to take up model making - but what subject should he choose to model? He had been given one of the original A1 treadle fretmachines, which he had restored to its original condition. "That's it!", he exclaimed, "I will have a go at making a model fretmachine". Obviously no plans were

Alan Cambridge proudly displays one of his model fretmachines

available, so Alan had to measure every part of his original machine accurately and scale it down to one third full size before spending hours in his workshop making the miniature version. He had never made a model before, but his skill as a tool and gauge maker gave him the necessary eye for detail and accuracy.

Encouraged by his first effort, Alan Cambridge joined the North Norfolk Model Engineer Club and has had some success in exhibiting his models at various shows. He has won three silver medals at the International Model Engineer Exhibition, held each year at Olympia, London, and another silver medal at the Norwich Model Engineer Show. Every model is fully working and meticulously detailed.

Right: Little and large, a full size A1 treadle fretmachine and its little brother
Below: Four of Alan Cambridge's one-third scale model fretmachines and a lathe

THE COLLECTOR

A collector extraordinaire is Brian Williamson. Brian has been retired now for seven years from a transport firm, where he was transport manager and director. Previously he had been a lorry driver. Brian started collecting items connected with Hobbies in 1937, when his father bought him a second-hand Gem treadle fretmachine. He later acquired a hand fretwork kit, and he still has both in his collection. However, with family grown up and mortgage paid, for the last 20 years he has been more dedicated to his hobby and now collects anything connected with Hobbies - fretmachines, tools, fretsaw kits, construction kits, steam engines, catalogues and handbooks, *Hobbies Weeklies*; you name it and Brian has probably got an example in his collection! He has also widened his collection to include steam powered engines and other toys from many other manufacturers.

Fortunately his wife, Barbara, shares Brian's interest - she doesn't have much choice as the collection has taken over most of their home! But Barbara is not left out of the collecting world as she collects tin-plate toys.

However, Brian Williamson's real passion is for products made by Bowman Models, and he has a fine collection of steam and aero boats, steam engines and locomotives. He is a keen and active member of the Bowman Circle, which now boasts over 40 members, all dedicated to the preservation and restoration of examples of Geoffrey Bowman Jenkins' products of the late 1920s and the 1930s. The Bowman Circle produces a quarterly newsletter which keeps the countrywide membership informed and in contact. Once a year, in February, members meet at the Steam Toys in Action Exhibition at Leicester Abbey Pumping Station, where they stage working demonstrations of many Bowman models and display practically the entire Bowman range.

Brian also belongs to the Norfolk Internal Combustion Engine Society, and just like Eric Barnes and Alan Cambridge, he loves to exhibit his collection at steam engine rallies and exhibitions. He exhibits at around 20 exhibitions each year, travelling

Brian Williamson with a fine example of a Hobbies' steam tug (made by Bowman Models) - part of his collection of steam driven toys can be seen in the background

Brian Williamson (centre), holding an M135 stationary engine, discussing their father's steam products with Max Bowman Jenkins (left) holding an Aeroboat II, and Paul Bowman Jenkins, holding an Express Passenger Loco Model 234 and tender

the length and breadth of the country. Brian and his wife also enjoy giving talks about their collections to members of local organisations. The talks are so popular that they manage to squeeze in around 50 a year.

A self-taught engineer, when Brian is not out exhibiting, giving talks or hunting for new acquisitions, he can usually be found in his workshop bringing items in his collection back to pristine condition. Often this involves researching specifications and making the necessary parts so that a particular model can be restored to fully working order once again.

EPILOGUE

Eric Barnes, Alan Cambridge and Brian Williamson are typical of the tens of thousands of hobbyists who have received both satisfaction and enjoyment through their different connections with Hobbies. They have also given delight to those who have seen the results of their labours, or who have spoken with them and seen their enthusiasm for a firm which has an unbeaten record of service to young and old for well over a century.

Acknowledgements

In the research and writing of this book a great deal of assistance has been afforded by a large number of people. The author wishes to place on record his appreciation to all who have helped in any way, without their support The Hobbies Story would have been incomplete.

In particular, special thanks are due to the staff of Hobbies (Dereham) Ltd., especially Ivan Stroulger and Robert Stroulger, for their support and encouragement freely given, for making available all their historical material, answering seemingly unending questions, and tolerating frequent interruptions to their working day with good humour.

Special thanks are due to Michael Dunn for his assistance with research into the early days of J. H. Skinner & Co. It is due to his involvement that many details of the early history of the firm has been revealed.

Grateful thanks are extended to Bertram Harrison and Karen Powley for checking the manuscript and for helpful advice and constructive criticism.

Several research archives and historical resources have given considerable assistance, including Companies House, The Public Record Office, The Patent Office, Gressenhall Rural Life Museum, Ian Clarke at The Dereham & Fakenham Times Office, Dereham, The Eastern Daily Press, the staff of Dereham Library, and the City of Toronto Archives

The support and interest of a number of individuals has been tremendous. Many were former employees of Hobbies Ltd. Some have provided photographs or information, shared a kaleidoscope of memories, or just identified a person in a picture. Whatever their involvement their help has been very much appreciated. They include Joan and Francis Dove, Charlie Elliott, Brian Williamson, Derek Toyne, Eric Barnes, Alan Cambridge, Maurice Eglen, Robin Green, Patrick Spielman (USA), Janet Pawley, Basil Day, Ivy Money, Olive Lansdale, Josie and Vic White, Brian Siggins, Len Titmus, Susan Palmer, David Skinner, Marjorie Glover, Margaret Thomas, Sylvia Gothard (USA), Doris Hatton, Ben Norton, Colin Chambers, Max Bowman Jenkins, Sue Martin, John Jones (The Bowman Circle), Ernie Basham, Elsie Rawling, Paul Fitt, Tony Aldiss

The illustration on page 25 (lower left), PRO Ref. BT 31/6930/48759, is reproduced by authorisation of the Public Record Office. Crown copyright material in the Public Record Office is reproduced by permission of the Controller of Her Majesty's Stationery Office

The photograph on page 104 is by the late George Ernest Swain, copyright The Norfolk Museums Service with funding provided by the Science Museum PRISM Fund

The photographs on pages 106 - 109 are reproduced by kind permission of the Eastern Daily Press

Last, but by no means least, sincere thanks to my wife, Shirley, who has become something of a "writer's widow" - she is assured that life does exist outside Hobbies!